OUR
ENGLISH COUSINS

BY

RICHARD HARDING DAVIS

ILLUSTRATED

NEW YORK AND LONDON
HARPER & BROTHERS
PUBLISHERS 1903

TO

STEPHEN BONSAL

CONTENTS

ILLUSTRATIONS

OUR ENGLISH COUSINS

I

THREE ENGLISH RACE MEETINGS

THE Derby, whatever it may have been to the English people in the past, seems to be chiefly patronized to-day by coster-mongers and Americans. I saw at the last Derby about forty thousand coster-mongers and gypsies, and some twenty thousand Americans, equally divided between well-known actors and the people you meet on the steamer. Of course there were other classes there, the idle rich and royalties, but they were not on the scene at all. They had as little to do with it as the Roman senators painted on the back drop in " Julius Cæsar," who remain stiff and dignified whatever befalls, have to do with the super senators who run up the stage crying " Kill, burn, destroy !" They formed a cluster of black hats in a corner of a grand-stand that rose as high as the Equitable Building—a wall of human beings with faces for bricks. The real

Derby crowd was that which stretched about this sheer wall upon Epsom Downs over miles and miles of dusty turf.

To approach the Derby in a proper frame of mind, and to get its full values, it is necessary to start sixteen miles away from it, and to draw near to it slowly and by degrees, and with humility of spirit. The spirit in which you return depends on different things—generally on a particular horse.

The Derby does not affect London town itself. I should like to be present at the public function which could. It does not overthrow it, and color it with blue and orange and black, as the football match does New York on Thanksgiving Day. It sprinkles it with a number of young men with field-glasses about their persons, and a few more coaches than usual, but that is all. You reach the Surrey side and Clapham Road before you note the difference. And from there on for sixteen miles you are not allowed to forget that you are going to the Derby. You go on a coach if you wish to see it properly. By it I mean the scene and the people, and not the races, which are a very small part of it, and which are like all other races in that the wrong horse comes in first. Clapham Road begins at the other end of Vauxhall Bridge, and as your coach swings into it on a trot you take your place in a procession, and only trot thereafter by accident.

This procession is made up of coster-monger carts; coaches with ringing horns and clanking harness; omnibuses, gay with enamelled advertisements; open trucks, carrying kitchen chairs for seats; hansoms, with hampers on top and mosquito nettings in front; and drays and vans and every make of wagon known to the London streets, from the Mile End Road of Whitechapel to the Mile of Hyde Park. To watch this procession on its way thousands of men and women line the two sidewalks and fill the windows of houses, the family, on the first floor, dressed for the occasion, and the nurse-maids and house-servants hanging out of the windows above them. These latter are amused or envious, as the case may be, and express themselves accordingly.

In the procession the coster-monger predominates. There is generally not less than six of him in one cart, with the poor little "moke," as they for some unknown reason call their donkey, almost invisible, save for his ears and his little legs, that go pluckily twinkling in and out from beneath the legs of his owner, which are stretched along the shaft and encircle his neck.

"Six men and only one donkey!" some one exclaimed to a coster after the races.

"And why not?" said the man. "We all on us 'ad whips."

The London coster is quite as typical in his

way as the London policeman. He wears a white
and blue dotted kerchief as the badge of all his
race, and a high-cut waistcoat and a full long-
tailed coat, both strung with pearl buttons as
closely as they can be sewed together. If he is
very smart he has his trousers slashed like a Mex-
ican vaquero's, with a triangle of black velvet and
more pearl buttons. This is his unofficial uniform. Many of the gypsies wear it too, and it is
all the more picturesque because it is unofficial.
He pays more than he can afford for one of these
suits, and they are handed down from father to
son, and so in their time see many Derbys, and
Sunday outings at the Welsh Harp, and bank
holidays. He leaves Farrington Road or Spitalfields or Whitechapel at four in the morning of
Derby day, and so reaches it about one in the
afternoon, after many halts. If he is a good coster, one who jumps upon his mother but seldom
and only beats his wife when drunk, he takes the
" missus " and the " nipper " and two or three
pals with him. If he is not married, he gives
the seat of honor to his sweetheart, or his " do-
ner," as he calls her. Her badge of office is a
broad silver chain with a large silver locket at-
tached, and a bonnet. She can also be told by
the way she bangs her hair. The silver chain is
inevitable; the bonnet is wonderful. The coster
girls pay for these latter a sixpence a week on
the instalment plan, and some of these bonnets

GOING TO THE DERBY

from Petticoat Lane cost as much as the milliners on Bond Street ask for theirs. But the coster girl gets much more for her money. Her bonnet is as broad as a sombrero, slanting down in front over her eyes and hair, and towering at the back above her head, covered with colored feathers and ribbons and velvet. This bonnet is as characteristic and local to the coster girls of the east of London as are the gold head-dresses to the women of Scheveningen.

It is necessary to give the coster-monger so much space because the Derby really belongs to him, although he does not grudge you the spectacle. He rather enjoys your being there. He considers catching your eye a sufficient introduction, and bids you with solicitude to be careful of your health, and asks, " Wot cheer, govenor?" or exclaims, ecstatically : " My! *wot* noice laidies you 'ave got along o' you ; *hain't* you? 'Er with the straw 'at in *particular*." Or he will stop suddenly in the middle of his song (for every wagon-load sings, so that as you go along you are steadily passing out of the burden of one melody into the rhythm of another), and standing up, cry, warningly : " Don't you listen to 'im, laidy. 'E's a-deceiven of you. It's just 'is gammon. Ahh! you sees, I knows you."

There is a great deal of this sort of thing. It is extremely funny, or rough and vulgar, if you like, but that is really no reason why Englishwomen of the better class should not see it, as none of them apparently have done. That, however, touches on a national characteristic which would take very long to explain, even were it not to me, at least, still unintelligible.

After two hours you draw away from the solid rows of suburban villas, with immortal names painted on their very little door-posts, and drive by parks, and into villages and past public-houses, in front of which hundreds of wagon-loads have been emptied, and where the occupants, having been refreshed and enlivened, are taking the stiffness out of their limbs by dancing on the very dusty village green, the "doners" in their young men's Derby hats, and the young men in the marvellous bonnets aforesaid. It is the noisiest and the best-natured of crowds, and the thirstiest, for the public-houses apparently are not frequent enough, and many wagons carry their own kegs of ale on temporary tables running down the centre, upon which the occupants sprawl, lean, and pound with their pewter mugs.

The commons and parks give way to broad fields and bunches of trees and hedges, and the procession breaks into a trot and breathes the fresh air thankfully; or we pass between the high stone walls of some great estate, and can see the tennis-court from the top of the coach, and the owner and his friends, even at this early hour, taking tea, which in England is like a motion to

adjourn. Even this far from town small boys, very red of countenance and covered with dust, accompany us on our way, turning cart-wheels or somersaults, and landing heavily on their backs, only to scramble up again and run after us to call, "Throw us your mouldy coppers, sir," or "'Ope you'll pick the winner, sir." At one place hundreds of orphans, in the uniform of the asylum to which they belong, are ranged behind a hedge under the care of sweet-looking teachers, and cheer wildly and continually, like a mob in a play, apparently at the prospect that some one at least, if not themselves, is going to enjoy himself. And men throw coppers, for which they scramble. It struck me that all the dear little girls in mob-caps, and the sweet little boys in regimentals playing so bravely in the asylum band, were learning a very curious lesson along that dusty highway, and that making beggars of them, and objects of careless pity from such a mob, would be hardly worth in years to come the few pennies which the day brought in.

To many of the crowd the Derby was an old story, and to wear away the hours they played cards on the tables placed in their vans, or danced up and down the confined limits of the wagon, while the others beat time on their knees. The good-nature is the most marked feature of the day, and quite well worth remarking when one considers that thousands of drivers are handling from four horses to one donkey each, and that each is trying to get ahead of the one immediately in front, and that each thinks his particular animal is best entitled to take and to hold the right of way.   Nothing, I think, speaks more highly of the Englishman's inborn knowledge of driving, whether he be a butcher-boy or Arthur Fownes, than this procession, three deep and sixteen miles long, on Derby day, with not a wheel gone nor a broken shaft to mark the course.

It is one o'clock before you leave the cultivated lands behind, and toil slowly up the steep hill to the downs, where the white dust rises suddenly like a mist and shuts out the rest of the world, leaving you in a white cloud, which blinds and suffocates you.   It makes you understand the mosquito nets in front of the hansoms and the blue and green veils around the men's hats.

It is a dust which conceals everything from view except the rear of the coach just in front and the flashes of light where the sun strikes on a piece of brass mounting.   It is like moving through a fog at sea.   One hears the crack of the whips and the creaking of wheels and leather all around, and the half-hearted protest of some guard on his horn, but one can only imagine what the dust hides, and comes out of it on the top of the downs as out of a Turkish bath, gasping and tearful, and wondering if those other people know how white and bedraggled and hag-

gard they look. The top of the downs is one
vast encampment — an encampment without apparent order or government, with every dust-
covered hedge in sight lined with picketed horses
and donkeys, and with hundreds more grazing
along lines of rope which early risers have stretched
for your convenience and their possible profit.
You must pass through a mile of this impromptu
stabling before you reach the race-track proper,
and between rows and rows of carts resting upon
their shafts, and hansom - cabs with the driver's
seat pointing skyward, and omnibuses abandoned
for the time to gypsies and hostlers. It is a
bivouac as great as that of an army corps. In
the centre of these open-air stables rises the grand-
stand, with its back towards London. It is the
highest grand-stand in the world, and the people
on the top of it cannot be recognized from the
ground even with an opera - glass. It faces one
end of a horseshoe track—a turf track, with stout
rails on either side of it. In the centre of this
horseshoe track is a valley ; and this valley, and
the track, and the downs beyond the horseshoe
track, are covered for miles with what looks like
a succession of great and little circuses and their
accompanying side-shows. There is not a row of
booths here and a bunch of tents there, but long
irregular avenues and streets built of booths and
flag-covered tents, with canvas pictures for walls,
stretching on beyond one another for a mile, like

a fighting line of old battle-ships with all their canvas set and all their signals flying; and in among these are thousands of people pushing and shoving and moving in black blocks and streams and currents, with a soldier's scarlet coat or a gypsy's yellow shawl showing for an instant, and then disappearing again in the ocean of black heads and white faces.

The Derby is quite free—at least, unless you mount the monster grand-stand, or go inside the enclosure between it and the track; but the rest is as free as a Lord Mayor's show, and on the day that I was there sixty thousand people availed themselves of this freedom. In a country given to spectacular exhibitions—Wimbledons, jubilee processions, boat-races, naval reviews—the Derby strikes one as quite the most remarkable thing of this sort that the English do, and they do them all particularly well. In no other country, I believe, do sixty thousand people travel sixteen miles to camp out around a race-track, and then break up camp and march back again the same night.

As a matter of fact, they do not all march back the same night. The gypsies and the fakirs, and hundreds of others around the training-stables (for the racing at Epsom Downs lasts a week), remain overnight, and this encampment, with the fires burning in the open air and the lights showing from under the canvas, makes as

AT THE DERBY

weird and wonderful a scene as that of the Derby
day itself. But in the morning this sleeping
bivouac rouses itself, and the tents go up as
easily as umbrellas, and an army of people crowd
the track and the grounds as thickly as the City
Hall Square is crowded on the night of a Presidential election. The coaches face the grand-
stand from the opposite side of the track. They
are packed as closely together as the omnibuses
in front of the Bank of England, so that one
could walk for half a mile from one to the other
of them without once touching the ground. The
first which come of these take the best places,
and the last are crowded in on them by the servants and the unemployed, who take out the
leaders and shove with the wheelers until they
have locked wheels with two other coaches, and
have apparently entangled themselves forever.
These coaches form a barrier three rows deep
along the course, and the dresses of the women
on top of them, and the luncheons, before their
pyramids are demolished, make the place look
like a succession of picnics in mid-air.

Back of these, down the valley between the
curves of the horseshoe, are tents and the rings
where wooden horses circle and prance, and railroad cars which mock the laws of gravity, dash-
ing up and down wooden hills, and where there
are shooting-galleries and boxing-booths and
swings, and rows after rows of gypsy wagons

2

(little green and red houses on wheels, with a pair of steps at the back like a bathing-machine), and solid phalanxes of shouting book-makers. These last stand in couples, dressed ridiculously alike, as a guarantee that they do not intend to lose themselves in the crowd, and with banners behind them to tell who they may be, from whence they come, and what a very old and trustworthy firm theirs is.

"Good old Ted Mark," and "Splasher Getters of Manchester"; "Diamond Jack of Birmingham"—"Fair play, quick pay, and civility to all" is his motto—and "Ikey Kennedy, the Music Hall pet," in a gilded four-wheel wagon, with his portrait in oils on the sides. There are dozens of such wagons and hundreds of book-makers. Some in white flannel caps, clothes, and shoes, or all in red silk with red silk opera-hats, others in evening dress with broad sashes spangled with bright new shillings like shirts of chain armor, and others in velvet or Scotch plaids. They are grotesque, loud-voiced, red-faced, and each couple identical in appearance, even to the flower in the button-hole and the scarf-pin. They will take anything from a shilling to a five-pound note, and they are given a great many of both.

But if you would get something for your money other than a ticket with "Lucky Tom Tatters of London" printed upon it, you can throw wooden balls at cocoanuts in front of a screen, or at wood-

THE WELSHER

en heads, or at walking-sticks, and perhaps get one of the cocoanuts, or a very bad cigar. You can also purchase a purse in which you have seen a gentleman in a velveteen coat put a sovereign, which is not there when you open the purse, or bet on which one of three cups the little round ball is under, or buy wooden doll babies with numerous joints to stick in your hat-band, or colored paper flowers and feathers to twine around it, these latter being traditional. People always put doll babies in their hats after the Derby— you can see them in Frith's picture; "it has always been done," they will tell you, if you ask, and that is all the reason you can obtain, or that you desire if you are a good Englishman. There are also numerous venders of tin tubes and dried pease, with which joyous winners on their way home pepper the necks of the helpless footmen on the back of the coach in front, and of pewter squirts filled with water with which they refresh-en the dust-covered " bobbies "; or, if you are a sportsman, you can watch a prize-fight which is always just about to begin, or shoot at clay pipes with a rifle, or try your strength by pounding a peg into the ground.

These are all very moderately priced pleasures, but there is much you can get for nothing at all. You do not have to pay to see the clown on stilts walking above the heads of the crowd, and frightening Eliza by putting one leg over her shoulder

and trusting that she will not jump the wrong
way ; or to see the man who allows any one in
the crowd to break with a sledge-hammer the
rocks which he holds on his breast. and who jumps
up unharmed and dashes after the dissolving au
dience with his tattered hat.

You see so much to entertain you on the
grounds that you forget about the races, although the sight from the coach is, in its broader
view, quite as amusing and impressive as the one
you obtain by pushing through the crowd.   Instead of moving about to see other people. the
other people come to call on you, chiefly musi-
cians of several nationalities, who sing sentimental songs sentimentally to the young women on
the next drag, who try to pretend they do not
know that they are being made to look ridiculous; and little yellow-haired girls on stilts, who
seat themselves on the box, and draw their stilts
up out of the way, and sing, " I'm er blushin' bud
of innercence ; papa says I'm a great expense ",
and troops of burnt-cork comedians who pretend
they know the people on the coaches, and who
flatter the weak in spirit by crying: "Ahh! glad
to see your lordship 'ere to-doiy.   I 'ain't forgot the 'arf-crown your lordship give me when
your lordship won that pot of money off King
Remus, Kemton Park Waiy.   Your lordship al-
lus wos a good one at pickin' a winner.   Now,
wot can we sing at yer lordship's command ter-

day?" At which his lordship, being a real-estate agent from Chicago, is extremely pleased, and commands his favorite melody.

There are a great many Americans at the Derby. It is something of which they have all heard. and in consequence want to see. An Englishman has also heard about it, but that does not necessarily make him want to see it.

There are some things there which no one cares to see—men fighting in the dirt for the chicken bones some groom has scraped off a plate and thrown between the wheels, and men who, when some one on the coach, seeing this, hands them decent food in a decent way, tremble all over as a dog does when you hold up a stick, and choke the food into their mouths with one hand while the other wasted one is stretched out for more, and men and boys sleeping heavily under the very feet of the crowd, worn out with the endless noise and excitement and the sixteen-mile walk and drink, and the young bank clerk who came overdressed, and was suddenly beset on all sides, and who now stands stunned and silly with empty pockets and a hole in his scarf to show where his pin had been. Or one sees a quick congestion of the crowd in one spot, and policemen making through it like men through water, arm over arm, until they meet around and rescue some poor wretch of a book-maker who has tried to sneak away from his debts, and upon whom one of his creditors, knowing that the law of England will not recognize a gambling debt, has called down the unwritten law of the race-track, and has hurled the cry of "Welsher!"—an awful word, that means nothing to us, but which sometimes on an English race-course means death from man-handling. And the fellow is run out into the track trembling with terror and clinging to the officers about him, with his tawdry suit of velvet torn from his back, and his face and naked shoulders covered with sweat and dust and the blood that shines brilliantly in the sunlight, all his blatant, noisy swagger gone, and with nothing left but an awful terror of his fellow-men. When Englishmen used to deprecate the sad prevalence of lynch-law in some parts of my own country, I used to ask them if they had ever heard a man cry "Welsher" in England, and they would fall back on the evils of our protective tariff and of our use of ice-water at dinner.

The races at the Derby are very beautiful examples of how grand a spectacle a horse-race can be. I can only speak of them as a spectacle, and not knowingly in sporting phraseology, because a compositor once made me say that the odds were "60 to 0," and a great many clever sporting editors, whose experience was limited to Guttenburg and Gloucester, and several English touts for the racing-stables that advertised in their papers, pointed out by this how little I knew. Until

these gentlemen spoke, I had supposed I knew
something of horse-racing in several countries; I
had certainly paid for my experience. But since
then I have avoided writing of horse-races, except
as a picturesque and pretty institution.

What first puzzles one at the Derby is where
the horses are going to find room to run, for

THE LAST HORSE

the track is blocked with the mob, which stands
doubtfully fingering the sixpences in its pockets,
and listening to the young men who are selling
tips on the race to follow, and beseeching the
crowd about them to remember what they foretold at the Manchester races a year ago.

"*Did* I soiy Orleander would win? Did I? I arsk you now, as man to man, *did* I, or did I not? I *did*. Right, sir, I did. And the gents wot patronized me got a quid for every bob they 'ad up. I don't spend *moi* toime 'anging round pubs, *I* don't. *I'm* hup every mornin' on these 'ere downs a-watchin' these 'ere 'orses run, and *I* knows wot's wot, and it's all writ down 'ere in these 'ere pieces of paiper which I'm givin' away for a tanner." Mixed with these young men are evangelists with an organ on wheels, to the accompaniment of which they sing hymns. They are not the Salvationists, though one sees the red jerseys of these also, but soberly clothed, earnest-looking men, perfectly impassive to the incongruity of their surroundings, and fervent in their hope of accomplishing some good. They have as large a circle about them as has the tipster, and they are too familiar a sight wherever many people are gathered together in England to be either scoffed at or encouraged. But when the bell rings, all of these—tipster, evangelist, and colored comedian—fly before the important business of the moment, and there is a rush to the rails, which men clutch desperately like wrecked mariners on a mast-head, and a sudden overflow among the carriages as the mounted police ride slowly along the length of the track, leaving a clear, broad, green road behind them.

And then the horses canter up the course, and

come back again with a rush of colors and strain-
ing necks amid what is almost, for so large a
multitude, complete silence. Englishmen do not
make themselves heard as does a racing crowd in
America. The most interesting effect in the race
to one who is looking up the track, and who is
not interested in the finish, is what seems to be
a second race, as the crowd breaks in after the
last of the horses and sweeps down the track,
making it appear shortened behind as the horses
move forward.

When it is all over there is the desperate
hurry of departure, the harnessing up of fright-
ened horses, and the collecting of the stray members of the different coaching parties, and a great
blowing of horns and cracking of whips, and
much inelegant language, and long and tiresome
waits of a quarter of an hour each, while the
great mob that arrived at different hours tries to
get out and depart at the same moment. But as
soon as the downs are cleared, and Clapham
Road is reached, the procession of the morning
is reformed ; the crowds, only greater in number,
line the way on either side, and there is much
more singing and much more blowing of horns
and playing of accordions and airy persiflage.
The coster does not object to making himself
look ridiculous. He rejoices intensely in a false
nose and a high paper cap. He would not feel
that he had enjoyed the day or done it proper

honor if some one in his party did not sing or
play the accordion, and if all of them did not
wear plumes in their pot hats. We have nothing which exactly corresponds with this at home ;
the people of the east and west sides, when they
go off for a day's holiday, do not make themselves ridiculous on purpose. If one of their
party wore a false nose, or a red and yellow hat
two feet high, or stuck doll babies all over his
person, he would be frowned upon as being too
" fresh." The day is not complete to the East-
Side tough here unless he helps to throw some
one off the barge, or thrashes the gentleman who
wants to " spiel " with his girl. And the Englishman of the lowest class is much more musi-
cally inclined than his American brother. From
the downs to High Street, Whitechapel, there is
one continual burst of song—the songs, as a rule,
it is interesting to note, being those which a man
of an entirely different class had written for audi-
ences of as wholly different a class, but which
were hailed and adopted unanimously by the people of the class about which they were written.
I refer to Albert Chevalier and his coster-monger
ditties. One sees the same thing in the way the
British soldiers in India sing Mr. Kipling's bar-
rack-room ballads, and the zeal with which the
inhabitants of Cherry Street have adopted Mr.
Braham's " Maggie Murphy's Home."

Many of these vocalists fall by the way-side,

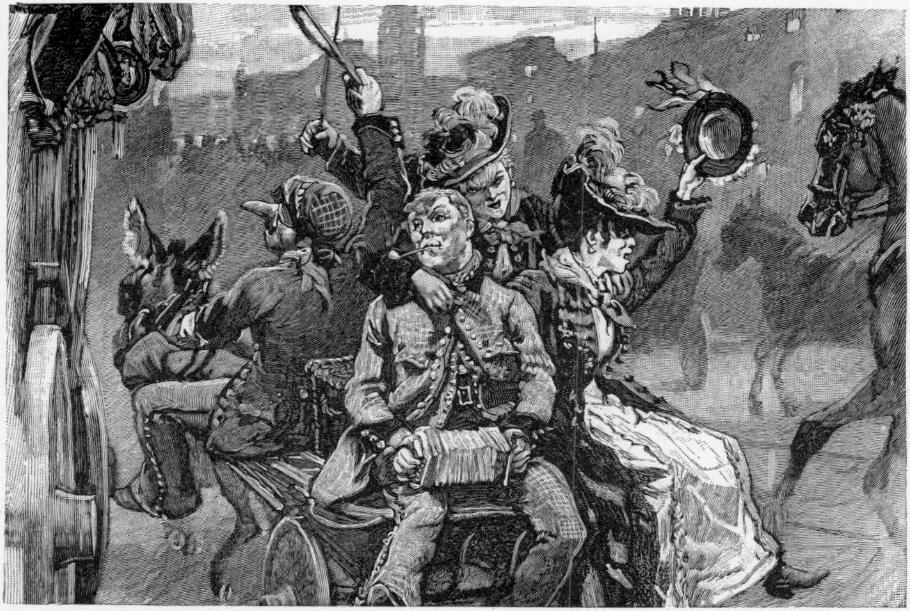

RETURNING FROM THE DERBY

under a hedge or against the walls of a public-
house, and the waits at these places become
more general and more ·frequent, and so it is
quite dark before you reach the asphalt again,
and find the streets ablaze with light and rimmed
with black lines of spectators and beggars, who
hope you have had a lucky day, and who en-
treat, with a desperation which recognizes this
to be the last chance for another year, that you
will throw them what remains of your "mouldy
coppers."

One finds the Cup day of Royal Ascot a somewhat tame affair after the rowdy good-nature
and vast extent of the Derby. It is neither the
one thing nor the other. There is rather too
much dust and too frequent intrusions of horses
upon the scene to make it a successful garden-
party, and there are too many women to make
it a thoroughly sporting race meeting. There
seem to be at least four women—generally twins,
to judge by their gowns—to every man. The
crowd that makes the Derby what it is, is only
present at Ascot on sufferance. The smart people, to whom Ascot primarily and solely belongs,
have all the best places and the best time; but
even the best time does not seem to be a very
good time. They all appear to be afraid of
mussing their frocks, which, when they have so
many, seems rather mean-spirited. There is a

track at Ascot over which horses run at great
speed at irregular intervals, but nobody takes
them seriously. One is either back in the royal
enclosure taking tea, or behind the grand-stand
on the lawn, quite out of sight of the track, or
lunching on the long line of coaches facing it, or
in the club and regimental tents back of these,
where, for all one can see of it, the race might
be coming off in Piccadilly. Every well-known
regiment has its own luncheon tent, with its
soldier-servants in front, the native Indians in
white and red turbans and the sailors being the
most successful. Many of the London clubs
have their tents also, and the pretty women, and
the big, narrow-waisted young men, all of whom
look and walk and dress alike—even to the yellow leather field - glass over the right shoulder,
which never comes out of its case — pass from
tent to tent, and from coach to coach, and from
the Enclosure to the grand-stand throughout the
whole of the day, seeking acquaintances and
luncheon, and tasting horrible claret - cup and
warm champagne. The Ascot races in '92 were
under the especial charge of the Earl of Coventry,
who, as master of the Queen's buck-hounds, had,
among other duties, that of refusing the applications of five thousand people for a place in the
Enclosure. This in itself must be something of
a responsibility, although it is likely that after
one has refused three thousand, the other two

thousand would not weigh on one's mind. It is also his duty and pleasure, when the court is not in mourning, to ride at the head of a group of richly attired gentlemen leading the royalties in their carriages.

This is a very pretty sight. The horses are very fine, and the "pink" coats very red, and Lord Coventry is, as he should be, the ideal of an English gentleman M. F. H. He only clears the track once; after that the ordinary mounted police perform this service, which is a somewhat superfluous duty, as the crowd go on with their own pursuits whether the track is clear or not. The Ascot gowns are probably the most striking effect of the day; a woman would recall one or two of them, but to a man they appear as a dazzling whole; they are the first and the last thing he sees; they force themselves upon him before anything else, as the multitude of hansom-cabs on a London street press on the eye before you recognize which street it is. They are not so beautiful or individual as are the gowns at the annual steeplechase at Auteuil; they would naturally not be, as the toilettes there are worn by Frenchwomen.

To the American there must always be something delightful in the idea of the Enclosure; but the reality is a trifle disappointing. He has, of course, outgrown the idea that royalties look differently from other people, but such an aggregation of social celebrities penned up, as it were, and on view to such an immense mob, seems to promise something less conventional. But it is interesting to hear the present bearer of a very great name fuss and fret because there are two and not three lumps in his tea, and to find that the very much made-up lady is *the* professional beauty, and *not* the young and very beautiful one who is laughing so heartily at a song of a colored comedian on the other side of the rail, and that she in turn was once a clergyman's daughter and is now a Personage indeed, and "walks in" before all the other great ladies and professional beauties and the young girl friends of her own age with whom she once used to play tennis and do parish work. It is also curious to consider that "only a brandy-bottle" stands between a shy little man and a title which is written up in bronze from Hyde Park corner to Westminster Bridge, and that the "black man," who is not at all black, in the ill-fitting gray frock-coat, is a prince of half of India, and that the very much bored young man who is sitting down while three women are standing and talking to him is a manufacturer's son who is worth a million pounds sterling. It is also interesting to hear the policemen tell the crowd outside the fence that they must not even "touch the railing." It makes you think you are at a circus, and listening to the keeper warning the group in front of the lion's cage. I really could not see what harm it would have done had they happened to touch the railing itself, especially when it was the fault of those behind who were so keen to see. And it is only fair to say that the lions behaved admirably, and were quite unconscious of the presence of so many awe-stricken spectators. That is all that saved it from being ridiculous on both sides of the barrier.

I do not think that royalty looks well in the garb of every day, and in the sunlight to which we can all lay claim. Its members should be reserved for functions and dress parades and levees. Their appearance in high hats and in jewels worn with cloth walking-dresses is artistically and politically wrong. It is much better not to have royalty at all than to have a democratic royalty which stops to laugh at Punch and Judy shows, as did George III., or goes to smoking-concerts, as do some of his descendants. Such conduct may endear royalty to the hearts of the people, but it is extremely annoying to the visiting American. Royalty is either royal or it is nothing; and when it steps off the red plush and walks over to Tattersall's to back Orvieto, it loses its only excuse and its only interest.

What impresses you most about Henley is the way in which every one contributes to make it what it is. It is not divided into those who are

looked at and those who look on. Every one
helps, from the young man in the blue coat and
the red ribbon of the Leander Club, who lounges
on the house - boat, to the perspiring waterman,
with his brass shield and red coat, who ferries
you from one bank to the other. The chance
spectator gives just as much to the scene as does
the winner of the Diamond Sculls. Every one
and every boat-load is part of a great panorama
of color and movement, some giving more than
others. Letty Lind, of the Gaiety Theatre, for
instance, under her lace parasol in the Gaiety enclosure, is more pleasing to look at than the stout
gentleman who is bumping everything within
reach of his punt, and who is kept busy begging
pardons from one end of the course to the other;
but even he makes you smile lazily, and so contributes to the whole.

You are impressed, as you are at so many of
the big English out - of - door meetings, with the
system and the order of the thing, and with the
rules which govern your pleasure, and the fact
that the rules which control the Henley week
are as strictly in force as those which govern the
Bank of England, and are quite as excellent.
There is no scrambling for places, nor mixture
of the good with the bad, and the speculator,
who does all he can to spoil every successful
meeting in America, from the football matches
and the Horse Show to a Paderewski recital, is

AT HENLEY

unknown.   A governing committee, or board of
trustees, or some such important body, sit in
conclave long before Henley week, and receive
applications from clubs for places along the bank,
and from families for portions of the lawns, and
from the owners of house-boats for positions on
the course.   And the board of trustees decide
who shall go where and which shall have what,
and the lordly house-boat and the humble fakir
who asks room on the opposite bank for his
cocoanut-stand are treated with equal consideration.   And so when you come down from town
in your flannels, prepared to be pleased and to
enjoy yourself, you find the scene set, and the
ushers in their places, and your seat reserved for
you.   That is the great thing about England—
its law and order, which keeps the hired carriages
out of the Row, which arrests you for throwing
an envelope out of a hansom-cab, and which con-
trols the position of your canoe at Henley.   In
America it is every one for himself.   In England
it is every one for every one else, and though the
individual may occasionally suffer, the majority
rejoice.   It may annoy you to find that you must
not anchor your launch to a house-boat, and leave
it there while you walk about on the turf; but if
it is left there it annoys hundreds of others who
need the room it takes, and so when you return
you will find that the river police have removed
it, and tied it up at some place where lost articles

are classified and cared for. This hurts your feelings, but it is good for the public.

The racing is a very small part of Henley. It
must necessarily be so when two boats only can
row at the same time, and when the advantage
of position means an advantage of two lengths
to the crew which pull under the shelter of the
house-boats. An arrangement so absurd as that
cannot be considered as coming under the head
of serious sport. Henley is a great water picnic,
not a sporting event; it is the out-of-door life,
the sight of the thousands of boats and thousands
of people in white and colors, all on pleasure bent,
and the green trees, and beautiful flowers of the
house-boats, and the colored lanterns at night and
the fireworks, which make Henley an institution.
It strikes one at first as being very small, as it
really is, much smaller than the name and fame
of the race and place lead one to expect.

You enter into the spirit of Henley when you
get your ticket in town, and find hundreds of
young men and maidens crowding the platform,
and dressed as no one would dare to dress in
New York city — in the most barbarous blazers
and brilliant boating suits—the sort of garments
men or girls might have worn a few years ago at
the Pier or at Bar Harbor, but which they would
certainly not expose to the stares of Broadway,
or to the criticisms of the idlers around a railroad
station. America is a fine free country in many

THE HENLEY PANORAMA

ways, but England is much more free in one, and allows her subjects or the strangers within her gates to dress as they please, and where they please. Hundreds more of such holiday-looking beings met the special trains at Henley station, and from that on you see no more round hats, or black coats, or varnished boots. The whole boating fraternity of the Thames seems to have been turned into the queer, quaint town, with its crooked streets and more crooked red roofs, and every one is sunburned and comfortable-looking and happy.

From the big stone bridge to a point a mile below, the house-boats stretch along one bank, and green grass and high trees line the other, and on the river between are processions and processions of boats, so close that the owners touch with their hands; they move along in blocks, or pull out of the crush by stealing a tow from the boat just ahead. A skilful and agile athlete could cross the river dry-shod at places by stepping from one boat to another. The boats and their crews disappear and reappear like a shuttle in a loom, moving slowly in and out, or shooting ahead if they are small enough, and you catch a glimpse of a pretty face or a more than striking costume only to lose it again as another boat slips in the way like the slide in a stereopticon. Whether you look down upon it from a house-boat or are in the midst of it in a canoe, the effect is more brilliant and the changes more bewildering than are the advancing and retreating lines of any great ballet you have ever seen. And at night, even when you try to sleep, you still see the colors and the shining sunlight flashing on the polished wood-work, and the boats as they move in and out and swallow each other up.

The setting of the scene is very good. Nature has been the landscape-gardener of one bank with trees and gradually rising hills, and man has made the other brilliant with the long row of house-boats. A house-boat can be a very modest and barn-like affair, or it can suggest a bower of fresh flowers and a floating Chinese pagoda combined. Those at Henley are of this latter kind. Some of them were pink and white, with rows of pink carnations, or white and gold, with hanging vines of green, or brilliantly blue, with solid banks of red geraniums. Some of them were hidden entirely by long wooden boxes of growing flowers, which overflowed and hung down in masses of color to the water's edge, and all had gorgeously striped awnings and Chinese umbrellas and soft Persian rugs everywhere, and silk flags of the owners' own design flapping overhead. It is only a step along the gang-plank to the lawn, and so on down the line to the next open space, where some club has a bit of lawn reserved for it, and has erected a marquee, and brilliant standards proclaiming its name, and guiding the thirsty and hungry member to its luncheon-table.

There are possibly more profitable ways of employing one's time and more intellectual amusements, but you are very near to content when you fall back in a wicker-chair on the top of one of these water-houses, and feel the breeze lifting the awning overhead, and hear the trees scraping it with their leaves; and were it not for the necessity of getting up to watch two crews of young men pulling violently past at an unusual speed, the race-week at Henley would be quite ideal.

A GENERAL ELECTION IN
ENGLAND

HERE were a great many questions asked in Parliament that afternoon. They seemed unusually unprofitable and unusually numerous, the Irish members, as always, being the chief offenders. Every one else wanted to hear one question answered, a question which everybody in Great Britain was asking everybody else, and which only one man could answer. The one man rose at last, with dignity, or diffidently, or languidly, as his manner chances to impress you, and faced a House in which every seat was filled, from the front row of the opposition benches to the high seat behind the ladies' lattice. There were cheers from the government benches, and then a sudden and impressive silence. The First Lord of the Treasury broke this appreciative silence by a review of what had been done by the government in the past, what it hoped to do in the little time left to it, and what it would be forced to leave undone. "And," he added, "Parliament will probably dissolve not before the first part of such a week, nor later than the last part of some other week."

The members of the Conservative party, who were just as anxious as any one else to learn the date of the dissolution, and just as ignorant concerning it, looked blank at this, and the opposition laughed and cheered ironically, as though to admit that they recognized the official utterance as not only unanswerable, but no answer at all. But they took it good-naturedly, like men who do not mind being played with if they are played with cleverly. All but Mr. "Willie" O'Brien, who raises his hat and begs to inform the First Lord of the Treasury that, owing to the government's failure to push a certain Irish bill, he will, so far as within him lies, oppose the progress of all other measures, to which threat, delivered in a hoarse, angry whisper, the First Lord of the Treasury answers by a polite bow of the head and a gratified smile. Then the House emptied itself, and every one went away not a bit wiser than when he had come in.

A week later the dissolution came. One of the hundred differences between an election in

4

America and an election in England lies in the
greater length of time which must elapse before
the result of an English general election can
be decided. With us the election of a Congressman decides the success of that particular
individual, while in England the political faith
of the members elected decides of what political
complexion the government shall be, and from
which side the Prime Minister shall be chosen.
The result of this is that the election of each
and every member in England, no matter how
unimportant he personally may be, counts just
that much on one side or the other, and the
interest is almost as keen in gaining every new
seat whether the man who holds it is Mr. Balfour or the unknown son of his father.

This system of spreading the election over
so many days makes a general election much
more entertaining to the visiting American than
is our own, where the people vote for the President before sundown on one day, and know
whether he is elected or not, and whether the
government has changed hands, before midnight. The English make very much more of
a good thing when they have it than that. The
American has only one fierce, anxious day of excitement and doubt; the Englishman stretches
the excitement and doubt over two or three
weeks, and gives every one a chance to proph-
esy things, and explain them when they do

not turn out his way, and say, " I told you so,"
or, " I knew how it would be," or, "Wait until
you hear from the boroughs," and then, after
you have heard from the boroughs, " Wait until
you have heard from the counties," and to hedge
several times before any one knows exactly who
is or who is not coming into power. This is
the most important difference from a merely
physical point of view; the others are the absence of bribery at an English election, and
the number of people who work without hope
of " getting anything for it," and the absence
of processions and brass-bands.

I suppose the elections I saw in England at
the last general election were considered legal
enough, but I sometimes used to doubt it. I
had been brought up properly to recognize that
no man can hope to be elected without the support of enthusiastic young men with capes and
oil lamps, and a brass-band to every fifty men,
and every third band playing " Marching through
Georgia." I saw nothing of this in England, and
so I waited patiently to hear that the votes had
been thrown out and that some one in authority
had ordered a recount. As this did not happen
I am forced to believe that a brass-band is not
necessary at an election, though I still think it
makes it a little more sure. It is like being married at the Mayor's office instead of being married with ushers and bridesmaids and rice. I

suppose one is just as legal as the other, but I should be as sorry to go to Congress without having had a band play " See the Conquering Hero " as to be married without at least six ushers wearing my scarf-pins.

A general election in England is conducted by the entire people. There may be a Central Committee somewhere, as there is at home, but its work is not so conspicuous to the stranger as is the work of the first chance acquaintance he makes. Recall the most enthusiastic politician of your acquaintance during the late campaign, and multiply him by the whole population of Great Britain, and you obtain an idea of what a hold politics has on the people of England. By this I mean all the people, the voters and the non-voters, the gentleman who has thirteen votes in different counties and the young women of the Primrose League who have none, the landlord whose gates bar at his pleasure the oldest streets in London and the lodger who pays a few shillings for the back room.

Every class works for its party and for its candidate in its different way. Its way may be to address mass - meetings under the folds of the union - jack or to humbly address envelopes, but whatever his way may be, every one helps. As soon as Parliament ends, this interest, which has been accumulating less actively for some time, becomes rampant, and members fly north and

"YOUR CHAMBERS ARE INVADED"

south, taking their wives with them to sit upon
the platforms, and their daughters to canvass
the division, and their friends to make speeches,
and the London season puts up the shutters until it is over. In London itself the signs of the
times are various and many. You can see it in
the crowds about the newspaper bulletin-boards,
in the desertion of the Row in the morning, in
the absence of the white light which had been
burning over Westminster, in the placards on
the hoardings, and in the carts and broughams
filled with voters driving in elegance to the polls.
The sandwich men on Piccadilly have changed
their announcements of new plays and Van Beer's
pictures and somebody else's catsup to "Vote
for Bings," and you look down an irregular line
of "Vote for Bings" like the ghosts in Richard
III., until you decide that no matter who the
rival candidate may be, you will *not* vote for
Bings. The under-butler, in undress livery, tells
you that her ladyship has gone to the country to
help Sir Charles in his canvass, and will not be
back for a fortnight ; and men you ask to dinner
write you a week later from Ireland to say they
have been attending the Ulster Convention, and
speak of it as a much more important event than
your dinner; and your chambers are invaded by
Primrose Dames, who cause your landlady to
look upon you with suspicion, and who seem to
take it as a personal grievance and as an inten-

tional slight on your part that you are an American and not entitled to a vote.

So I, personally, left London and followed the campaign through the fortunes of one candidate. And as his canvass resembled that of others, more or less, I will try to show through it what an English election is like. My Candidate's fortunes were very pleasant to follow, because his canvass was conducted with much picturesqueness in the form of rosettes and outriders, and was full of incident and local color, the local color being chiefly red.

It might have been my luck to judge an English election by the efforts of a candidate unknown to the borough he wished to represent, who would have stood at the direction of the Central Committee, and who might have been *non personâ gratâ* to the electors of even his own party. In this case he would have put up at whichever inn favored his political conviction, whether it was the better one or not, and he would have canvassed the division as a stranger, and as a stranger have been treated accordingly. For, as you probably know, a gentleman who has lived in Wales may take a train across the country and stand for a division in Scotland, or *vice versâ*, just as Mr. Stanley, who has spent a great part of his life in Africa, stood for Lambeth, because the Central Committee of the Liberal Unionists assigned him to that division, and not because he was wanted there; indeed, as was apparent later, he was not. But My Candidate stood for a county division where his people had been known for hundreds of years, and where he had been known for at least thirty, where the game-keeper remembered having handed him his first breech-loader, where the hunting set who follow the Duke of Rutland's hounds spoke of him as a "clinker" across country, and where the head of the family was the Lord Lieutenant of the county, and the owner of a great mansion which was familiarly particularized for seventy miles around as "the House." And while all this and all that pertained to it did not make his calling and election sure, it did make his efforts to render that election sure of peculiar interest to the visiting American.

My first intimation that I was to follow My Candidate's fortunes was an invitation delivered by himself in person during a luncheon in town, into the third course of which he plunged uninvited to ask if I would like to go down to a political meeting of his that night and have my head broken. Mr. Oscar Wilde was also included in the invitation because he happened to be there, but he showed a lack of proper sporting spirit, and, pleading an engagement, returned to the consideration of the fourth course. My host let me off, and My Candidate took me in a train to some place, where a carriage met us, and car-

ried us the rest of the way to a village with a
queer name. In that way was I pitchforked
into English politics. That night we spoke at
the school-house. I say "we" because for the
few weeks which followed I cast my lot in with
the Conservative party and My Candidate, and
though I did not speak but once, on which unhappy occasion I turned all the Conservatives of
sixty years' standing into rabid Radicals, I always
considered myself in the plural number.

We had a small audience. It was as large as
the school-house could hold, but it was small,
and it was phlegmatically and delightfully Conservative. The farmers and their wives sat on
the front row, with the young ladies from the
rectory and the local political agent. Back of
these were the agricultural laborers, who corre-
spond as a political factor to our sons of honest
toil, and who wore suits of white corduroy and
red ties, and who surprised one by looking exactly like the agricultural laborers in the *Chatterbox*
of our childhood and in the *Graphic* Christmas
numbers of to-day. They had red, sunburnt
faces, and a fringe of whiskers under the chin,
and hair that would not lie down. When they
were Conservatives they were nice and sober
and clean-looking, and kept their lips closely
shut while they observed us with bovine admiration and approval; but when they were Radicals,
they, by some curious mental process, became

strikingly unintelligent and boorish-looking, and
expressed their only interest in the proceedings
by howling " boo " or " yah." My Candidate ad-
dressed the loyal electors of the village in a happily keyed conversational tone. He made, on
the whole, a most satisfactory and clever speech,
and I learned for the first time how to say " hear,
hear !" in such a way as to convey the sound of
" 'ere, 'ere !" and the idea of marked approval and
deep conviction at the same time. And even
after I had heard him deliver the same speech at
four villages a night for a fortnight I still pre-
served my admiration for it, and, as I recall it
even now, I remember it fondly as a satisfactory
and clever oration.

We did not speak beyond ten minutes, and
then we made way for the political agent, and
bowed to our electors, and got into the carriage
again, and gave our driver the name of the next
place. I have followed the fortunes of politi-
cians in my own country from town-hall to local
assembly-rooms in much the same way, and I
have journeyed from the Pavilion Music-hall to
Islington and from Islington to the Surrey side
with Albert Chevalier and other great men of
the London music-halls, and I was reminded
during our drives from one queerly named village
to another more queerly named of both of these
former experiences, and yet there was a vast difference. There was the same slamming of the

carriage door, the same quick gallop of horses, and the same welcoming hurrah and glare of light and hand-clapping at the end of it, but My Candidate's road did not lie over greasy asphalt and between rows of lamps, but through hedges in full bloom and in the soft twilight of an English summer. We forgot our speech and the last placard of the opposition in the silence of the fields, and at the sight of the old-fashioned gardens and the hedges of hawthorn and the long single rows of feathery English trees, and we stopped discussing " one man one vote " to point out the spire of a village church or a cluster of thatched cottages with soft roof-lines broken with bunches of climbing-roses and curling smoke. I shall remember those long drives in the late twilight long after My Candidate has become a cabinet minister, and even after I have forgotten his satisfactory and clever speech.

The next place received us calmly, although we came into it at a gallop, and with the Candidate's dog barking excitedly from the carriage window. Old women, who could not vote, dropped us courtesies from the cottage half-doors; and their daughters, who could not vote either, waved their aprons, and ran by the wheels to wave their hands in the windows; but their good men, who *had* votes, kept their hands in their pockets and their pipes in their mouths, and scowled uncomfortably over the hedges, as though

"THEIR GOOD MEN, WHO HAD VOTES"

instinct told them to touch their caps, and the
Radical political agent had told them they must
do nothing so foolish. Our local agent, with a
union-jack in his button-hole, received us thankfully, for the gentleman then speaking had been
trying for the last hour to hold the meeting together until we came, and was getting more
hoarse as the crowd grew more noisy, and it had
become a necessity of night or Blücher. Then
the local agent, who is always a young man with
smooth hair and strong lungs, suddenly began to
jump up and down and to cheer frantically, as
though he had just discovered the Candidate's
arrival, and the meeting turned to look, and the
speaker said, "Thank Heaven!" and dropped into
his chair, breathing heavily. The Candidate's
speech was a little longer this time, because of
doubtful spirits in the audience who had to be
converted, and on account of their numerous interruptions. It struck me as a very noisy meeting, and I waited with some impatience to see the
noisiest one put out as an example and a warning
to the others; but no one was at all put out, not
even the Candidate. That was my first experience of a mixed political meeting in England,
and of the great and most curious institution of
"heckling." Later in the campaign I was not so
anxious to see the noisiest one put out as to as-
certain at just which point in the proceedings it
would be wisest for us to get out ourselves.

The next speaking-place was one of the largest in the division. It was strongly Radical. This was the place where the Candidate had promised me we should have our heads broken.

If you have ever attended a political meeting at home you will better appreciate how strange to an American must be a political meeting in England. The object of a meeting with us is to give the candidate and some of his political friends an opportunity of telling all of those who care to come and listen what his party proposes to do, what he proposes to do if he is elected, and to point out with damning frankness the corrupt and evil doings of the other party. Those who do not care to hear this remain away ; those who do, interrupt the proceedings only by begging the speaker to " let 'em have it," referring by this, of course, to the corrupt and evil other party. Any further effort on the part of the members of the audience to make antiphonal chorus of the meeting results in their being ejected forcibly and without sympathy or gloves. The result of this is that seldom any but Republicans attend a Republican meeting, and only good Democrats go to Democratic meetings, and every one departs having heard what he already knew, and more firmly convinced than before, in default of any testimony to the contrary, that his candidate and his party are the right ones. And he in time votes accordingly like a good citizen.

But the English look at this differently. The Briton's vote is a very precious thing to him, and he wants to know exactly who is going to get that vote, and why he thinks he should get it. So he goes to the meeting at which the candidate is announced to speak and asks him. This is called "heckling"; it is a Scotch word, and in Scotland is carried out with the careful and deliberate consideration which marks that people.

The Scotchman who invented heckling probably looked at it in this way. This man, he argues, wishes to represent my interests, he wants my vote: "the Scotch are no a wasteful folk," and I shall not give him my vote until I am convinced I am getting the best possible value for it. We read of an English candidate appealing to his constituents, and of one of the great English parties appealing to the country. Our candidates are not placed in any such bemeaning position. They are too proud to appeal to their constituents. The bosses give us our candidates and we try to feel thankful and vote for them, as we should, and there are no questions asked. But the unhappy English candidate is expected to give a reason for the faith that is in him to any one and every one who calls upon him so to do. This is heckling. Sometimes the privilege of heckling is conducted in good faith, but more frequently it is not. It has one great advantage, it teaches the unfortunate candidate to think while he is on his legs, and to keep his wits and his temper.

There was a man with a blue necktie. He was a most unpleasant gentleman, and he rose to ask questions at irregular moments with a pertinacity of purpose and a confident smile which no amount of howling on the part of the good Conservatives could dismay.

" Mr. ——, sir," he would say, " I 'ave a question I would like to put to you, sir. Did you, sir, or did you not, vote for the Impecunious School - masters Bill as presented on July 2, 1890?"

Now it was not at all likely that any of the Radicals present had ever heard of the bill before, or cared twopence about it if they had, but they saw the fiendish purpose of the question, and they howled accordingly, a triumphant, mocking howl, quite long and loud enough to drown any possible answer in case the Candidate had one to make, and sufficiently exasperating to make him forget it if he had. But the Candidate would smile easily, and raise his hands imploringly for silence, and then turn his head over his shoulder with a quick aside to his political agent, or to one of the other speakers, and whisper, fiercely, " Quick! look it up! what bill does the ass mean?" and then smile encouragingly on the heckler, while the political agent would thumb

"'GENTLEMEN,' THE CANDIDATE WOULD BEG"

over a Speaker's Hand-book, and whisper back, hidden by the Candidate's figure: "Introduced by Lord Charing, seconded by Paddington; lost on second reading, 64 to 14. You voted *for* it. It was a bill to subsidize county school-teachers." Then the Candidate, who had probably been taking tea on the terrace when the bill was introduced, and who had voted with his party at the division, and returned in time to say, "Two lumps, please," would smile cheerfully, and ask the heckler if he would be so good as to repeat his question, which the heckler judged was a subterfuge to gain time, and would repeat it in a more triumphant and offensive manner than before.

"Impecunious School-masters Bill? Oh yes," the Candidate would say. "Introduced by Lord Charing, I believe. Oh yes, a very excellent bill; seconded, if I am not mistaken, by Mr. Paddington," and then, turning to the political agent, "Am I right?" to which the political agent, after a moment's consideration, nods a decided assent. "I voted for that bill." All the Conservatives cheered, and the gentleman with the blue necktie sat down, rather red in the face, and scanning the notes, with which the Radical political agent who had sent him there had furnished him, with dawning distrust.

But we did not always triumph. Sometimes My Candidate would sit on a table, patiently

swinging one leg and rolling and consuming cig-
arettes for a half-hour before the room grew sufficiently quiet for a steam-roller to have been
heard around the corner. As exhibitions they
were the most unfair, the most cruel, and the
most unmannerly I have ever witnessed, and
they were the same in every division in England. It used to remind me of a thorough-bred
horse hitched to a post, with all the dirty little
curs in the village, knowing that it could not
reach them, snapping and snarling at his heels.

"Gentlemen," the Candidate would beg—
"gentlemen, do you call this fair play? Do you
call yourselves Englishmen? Do you— Oh, go
to the devil!" and he would roll another cigar-
ette and sit down on the edge of the table and
wait. When they were too hoarse to yell and
boo any longer, he would begin his speech again,
or would imitate the excellent example of one of
our Irish speakers, and call out in a breathing-
spell, "I can't talk against two hundred men,
but I can thrash any one of you here on this
platform." They always rose at this, not because
they knew he could or could not, but some latent
feeling of fairness would be stirred by it, and then
they would bid him have his say and "speak up."

I suppose the abuse has grown to the limit it
has reached to-day because the position in which
the candidate puts himself when he appeals to
his electors is the only one when he is a petitioner,

and not a superior being and a patron. In this country a candidate never dares to pretend that he is better than any one else, whether he has but his vote or is the President of his country. And so, when he goes forth to ask for votes, his attitude is unchanged; he is still, as he has always been, one of ourselves.

But you can see how different it must be in England. For months or years the candidate, especially a Conservative candidate, lives and moves in another atmosphere from that which his constituents breathe. He subscribes to their societies and golf and football clubs, and addresses them from the head of the table at dinners, and condescends to play cricket with them, and to give them a pass into the strangers' gallery to look down upon him with his hands in his pockets, his hat cocked over his eyes, talking familiarly to a cabinet minister. They stop trimming hedges to run and open the gate when he rides to the meet, or hurry from the shop to the sidewalk to take his order when his cart stops in front of the door.

And then on one day all this is changed, and their chance comes, and they take it. Their candidate returns to them heralded by posters, and a circular letter which begs a renewal of that confidence which he has already enjoyed, hoping he has pleased them in the past, and promising to be good, and even better, in the future, if they

will only send him back to that fine club in
Westminster again.   It is all very courteous and
friendly and dignified ; but the electors, like Mr.
Kipling's soldiers, know they are "no thin red
line of heroes," and that telling them they are
intelligent and free electors is not going to alter
the fact that for years or months they have been
touching their hats, and that it is now their turn,
and that the candidate is taking his hat off to
them.

You can hardly blame them.   They are not
intelligent enough to act as equals in the first
place, nor independent enough to be magnani-
mous at the last.   "Now, my good man," the
Candidate would say, "why do you make so
much noise ?   What have you got against me ?"
And the good man would squirm and scowl and
say, finally, "Ah, you're a gentleman, and we uns
ain't goin' to have no more gentlemen a-keepin'
us down ;" and then he would manifest his new-
born freedom by yelling "boo" for half an hour
while the gentleman bit his lip and raised his
hand wearily for silence.   I do not mean to say
that every meeting was like this, but half of them
were.   And it is only fair to say, also, that it was
not always the voters who made the most noise.
Half-grown boys or the navvies from the near
railroad works, with no other interest in the proceedings than the delight they took in annoying
the swell, often made the greater part of the riot.

"TOLD YOU SADLY, AS HE FIXED YOUR BATH"

But heckling is, for all that, the blot on the English election. It shows a cruel, brutal love of torturing something, even if that thing is a man. It is the bull-baiting of the present day.

As heckling is the thing the American can't understand or admire, so the Corrupt Practices Act and its workings is the feature of an English election which appeals to him as its greatest triumph and glory. It is quite safe to say that bribery, as we know it, is unknown in England. The laws are against it, the sentiment of the people is against it, and the condition of things at the present time is against it. The Corrupt Practices Act places the conduct of an election in the hands of one person, the political agent, who is made responsible for, and who must furnish an itemized account for, every penny spent during the campaign. Every voter of the opposition is virtually an auditor of that account, and proof of corruption in the slightest degree, if corruption has degrees, not only sends the political agent to jail, but loses the candidate his election.

It is interesting to remember that after this general election Mr. Frank C. James, the Conservative who was elected in Walsall, was deprived of his seat by the courts because he provided hat-cards or favors for his adherents. That is, if an English candidate should supply his friends with the buttons which are worn over here by the adherents of different men and parties he would be looked upon as a corrupt and bribe-giving miscreant, and lose his chance of sitting in the Lower House. Mr. Nathaniel George Clayton also lost his seat; his offence consisting in his having given a check to a Conservative, who used the money to organize a picnic. This was held by the court to come within the provisions of the act prohibiting treating. It is of no use to say to this that we also have laws to punish corruption. We have, and every one knows how seldom they are enforced, and how little public sentiment there is back of them to put them in motion.

In England there is as little possible reward for services rendered after the election as there is actual bribery for services rendered before the election. Indeed, the most remarkable thing to me about the English elections was the number of women and men who worked for the different candidates with no other incentive than the desire to see their man and their party win. The shopkeepers, after a long day behind the counter, worked in the committee-rooms until two in the morning, folding and mailing circulars and other campaign matter. The women of the village, led by the rector's wife, directed forty-five thousand envelopes in one week; and the ladies from the Castle rose early and canvassed the town in rain and storm to fill in the little slips with which the political agent had furnished them,

and which they forwarded to him at headquar-
ters before they went to sleep at night.   Gentlemen of many clubs deserted these clubs to travel
in open dog-carts over rough roads to speak at
noisy, heated meetings, to sleep in strange inns,
and to eat when and where they might.   No fly-
by-night theatrical company or travelling tinker
works harder or suffers more privations than does
the political speaker at an English election.   And
for what?   Not to get office, because the Member of Parliament has none to give.   Not to gain
notoriety, for his speeches are not reported; and
certainly not to make himself popular, for he is
lucky if he gets out of town with his carriage
windows and his head unbroken.   He is not a
very bright speaker, the average English gentleman.   He hems and hesitates, and deals largely
in figures which the Chancellor of the Exchequer,
were he present, might be able to contradict, but
which the agricultural laborer imbibes unques-
tioningly.   But he deserves the greatest possible
honor for the trouble he takes and for the spirit
which leads him to take that trouble, and which
shames the busy American gentleman who thinks
he has served his country well and sufficiently if
he remembers to register and who then pairs off
with some one else that they may both spend
Election Day in the country.   The gentlemen
who spoke for My Candidate came from all over
Great Britain.   Half of them were his personal

friends, and as many more utter strangers, who spoke for him because the Central Committee had asked them so to do, and who on the next morning hurried away to speak for some one else.

They were as various as the days of the year, and as entertaining. They came at all hours, un-heralded and unknown, some to remain at the House only overnight, to appear for a brief half-hour in the smoking-room, and to depart before we came down for breakfast, and others to re-main three or four days, and to furnish the House party with matter for infinite speculation and de-light.

The House party added an element to the campaign which was at least diverting. Its mem-bers were the drones in the hive. Some of them could not speak because they were members of the House of Peers, or because if they had spoken they would have gained more votes for the other side than the Candidate could afford to lose, or because they were Americans. But they lifted the strain of the canvass in different ways, and served to turn the Candidate's thoughts to light-er things, and to give him some one near at hand to abuse. It made an interesting picture at night, after the women had taken their candlesticks and the men had foregathered in the billiard-room, the non-speakers of the House party in their smok-ing-jackets amused or politely cynical, and plan-ning tennis matches for the morrow, and the

"THE WOMEN RAN INTO THE STREET"

speakers enthusiastic and self-important, covered with flecks of flying mud, and very hoarse, and all trying to tell at the same time of the success with which their oratory had been received by the intelligent electors of Pigley-on-Thames, or Little Market Leeping, or Pippingham Corner.

"You can't make too much of that," the London barrister would say, rocking from one foot to the other in front of the fireplace. "That's an argument which I use in every speech I make. That appeals to their pockets. What does the agricultural laborer know of home-rule, or care—"

"Ah, I think you're wrong there," the dissenting clergyman from Cork would interrupt. "Home-rule is the question. Now my experience is that they'll always listen to that. I find—"

"Well, they wouldn't listen to me," the Oxford graduate breaks in, gloomily. "They jolly well hooted me."

"Is that all?" laughs the Central Committee man, easily. "My dear boy, wait till you speak at Eppingham Commons. They chased me for a mile."

And so it would go on, with the Candidate sitting in the middle, sipping cold Scotch, and nodding his head to each in turn, and wishing they were all in bed, while the drones banged the billiard balls about and made mental notes for the amusement of the women-folk in the morning.

6

The court-yard was always filled with carts or traps or flies from the inn, or the bicycles of the telegraph messengers, and the table below-stairs was always set for these worthy people, and the table up-stairs always spread with what was breakfast for one man, and luncheon or dinner for another, or all three for the Candidate. They were most amusing, these elongated breakfasts, where a speaker would stop, with his plate in his hand, between the sideboard and the table to repeat a particularly fine flight of the night before, and the butler would wait impassively until the gentleman who had asked for more claret-cup had finished using his glasses to show the position of the Unionist stronghold in Ireland. It was politics all day and long into the night, from the early morning, when the man who valeted you told you sadly, as he fixed your bath, that " we " had lost three seats since the night before, until nightfall, when the last tired speaker came apologetically in from the darkness and assured us that he had saved the sixty votes of Midland Tooting by the greatest oratorical effort of his life.

The part the women play in an English election is one of the things which no American can accept as an improvement over our own methods. It may either amuse him or shock him, but he would not care to see it adopted at home. The canvassing in the country from cottage to cottage he can understand ; that seems possible

enough. It takes the form of a polite visit to
the tenants, and the real object is cloaked with
a few vague inquiries about the health of the
children or the condition of the crops, and the
tract - like distribution of campaign documents.
But in town it is different. The invasion of
bachelor apartments by young Primrose Dames
is embarrassing and un - nice, and is the sort of
thing we would not allow our sisters to do; and
the house-to-house canvass in the alleys of Whitechapel or among the savages of Lambeth, which
results in insult and personal abuse, is, to our way
of thinking, a simple impossibility. The English,
as a rule, think we allow our women to do pretty
much as they please, and it is true that they do
in many things enjoy more freedom than their
British cousins, but the men in our country are
not so anxious to get into office, greedy as they
are after it, as to allow their wives, in order to
attain that end, to be even subject to annoyance,
certainly not to be stoned and hustled off their
feet or splattered with the mud of the Mile-End
Road. Any one in England who followed the
election last year knows to the wife of which
distinguished candidate and to the daughters of
which cabinet minister I refer.

I have seen women of the best class struck by
stones and eggs and dead fish, and the game did
not seem to me to be worth the candle. I confess that at the time I was so intent in admiring

their pluck that it appeared to me as rather fine than otherwise, but from this calmer distance I can see nothing in the active work of the English woman in politics which justifies the risks she voluntarily runs of insult and indignity and bodily injury. A seat in the House would hardly repay a candidate for the loss of one of his wife's eyes, or of all of his sister's front teeth, and though that is putting it brutally, it is putting it fairly.

It would not be fair, however, if I left the idea in the reader's mind that the women go into this work unwillingly; on the contrary, they delight in it, and some of them are as clever at it as the men, and go to as great lengths, from Mrs. Langtry, who plastered her house from pavement to roof with red and white posters for the Conservative candidate, to the Duchesses who sat at the side of the member for Westminster and regretted that it threatened to be an orderly meeting. It is also only fair to add that many of the most prominent Englishmen in politics are as much opposed to what they call the interference of women in matters political as they are to bribery and corruption, and regard both elements of an electoral campaign with as pronounced disfavor. The reply which the present President of the United States made to those enthusiastic and no doubt well-meaning women who wished to form leagues and name them after his wife, illustrates the spirit with which the interference of women

"THE LADIES IN THE WINDOWS OF THE INN"

in politics is regarded in this country.   But then
it is a new thing with us, and it is only right to
remember that from the days of the Duchess of
Devonshire's sentimental canvass to the present,
English women have taken a part in general elections; that there is a precedent for it; and when
you have said that of anything English, you
have justified it for all time to come.   It is,
after all, like the tariff, a "local issue," and the
young American girl who would not think it
proper to address men from a platform and give
them a chance to throw things at her must remember that the English girl would not give the
man she knew a cup of tea in the afternoon unless her mother were in the room to take care of
her.   And I am sure the women in My Candidate's campaign almost persuaded me that they,
as the political agent declared, did more than
himself to win the election.   They did this by
simply being present on the platforms, by wearing our colors, or by saying a kind word here or
giving a nod of the head there, and by being
cheerfully confident when things looked gloomy,
or gravely concerned when the Candidate was
willing to consider the victory already assured.
As the young Boston Democrat who was of the
House party used to say to me, confidentially,
"If we had that girl to help us in America, I'd
be willing to run for Governor of Texas on the
Republican ticket."

The canvass lasted two weeks. They were
two weeks of moonlight rides at night from one
village to another, of special trains by day, and
speeches in clubs, at cross-roads, in the market-
places, and in the crowded, noisy school-rooms,
and they ended with a long drive, on the day
before the poll, of thirty miles through all the
villages. As we were good Conservatives and
people of high degree, of whom such things were
expected, we made these thirty miles behind four
white horses, with postilions in red jackets and
green velvet caps, and with long cracking whips.
It made me look back involuntarily for the pur-
suing parent, or ahead for the gentleman in the
gray caped coat and cocked hat who should have
waited for us at a cross-road behind pistols and
a black mask. The Radical Candidate made the
same final trip over the same route in a dog-cart,
driving tandem, with his sister beside him and a
groom at the back. We met at the principal
town on the road, and he pulled up smartly, and
he and our Candidate leaned over and shook
hands, and the sisters of the rival candidates
smiled sweetly at one another, and said, " What
a pity it is such a rainy day!" and we men raised
our hats stiffly and proudly, and the excited populace wept tears of joy. It was an historical moment, and gained both Candidates many votes.
We left our starting - point in a drizzling rain,
with the sisters of the Candidate in beautiful red

silk capes, and the Candidate in the open carriage, and with two of the "hangers - on;" as we
aliens from America or London were called, on
the box. And we all bowed and smiled for thirty
miles. The two on the box bowed to the pro-
spective voters back in the fields behind the
hedges, and we in the carriage to those at the
cottage doors, and so every one was included,
and the feelings of no possible voter were inten-
tionally hurt. Sometimes they appreciated the
honor done them and sometimes they did not.

At one place it was all blue, blue being the
Radical color in that division, and the streets
looked like the grand-stand at the Polo Grounds
when Yale has scored. They greeted us in this
village with curses and groans, and the women
ran into the street beating tin cans and trays
to frighten the horses, and made unladylike
faces and used unladylike language. We thought
it a most dirty and unpicturesque village, and
the postilions put their heads down and lashed
the horses into a gallop. But at the next place
and the next they had luncheons spread for
us, and everything was red and all the windows were hung with the Candidate's portrait,
and nice old ladies with red bows in their lace
caps bowed to us from the front windows, and
the maids waved flags from the doors, and the
constituents raced alongside in the mud and
made us feel very important indeed. The Can-

didate never properly appreciated the luncheons. He did not consider them important. But my brother and the other " hanger-on," who was a very smart youth in a long-tailed coaching-coat and a winning smile, used to help the cause along wonderfully. "You're very good," the Candidate would protest to the anxious host, " but I really cannot eat anything more. I have some friends outside, though—" Then he would call down the hangers-on from the box-seat as substitutes, and they would set cheerfully to work again, as though the effects of the luncheon of the last village had been washed away in the rain.

" I assure you, sir," the political agent would say, pounding the table, "that the meeting last night was the greatest—"

" I say," the one in the coaching - coat would interrupt, earnestly, " would you kindly pass the pigeon-pie? Thank you."

We had three luncheons before we reached B——, where we stopped two hours to rest the horses. B—— was the place where the votes were to be counted the next day, and strongly Radical. We found it very stupid waiting about after the exciting progress of the morning, while the horses were being baited, and so we wrote out a placard in the inn announcing the loss to Mr. Gladstone of four thousand votes in Mid-lothian, and put it up outside. I regret to say

"THE MOB SEIZED THE HANGER-ON"

that this placard, when viewed from a distance, read as though Mr. Gladstone had lost Midlothian. The line " four thousand votes at " was there, but it was written so very small that no one could make it out unless he got within a few feet of it, which some good Conservatives prevented by standing in front of it. But the Radicals reached it at last and tore it down, and while we remonstrated the hanger - on in the coaching-coat went into the inn to prepare another bulletin. The remonstrances drew the crowd around us, and the crowd began to hustle, which is not what we mean in America when we use that word, but is putting your shoulder against a man and shoving him. About three hundred Radicals began to do this, and the Candidate broadened his shoulders and braced himself, and the Conservative workers plunged into the mob to help, and everybody began to sway and push, and the ladies in the windows of the inn became anxious. The hanger-on in the meanwhile had prepared his duplicate placard, and two Conservatives helped him up on their shoulders that he might nail it high above the reach of the mob. But the mob seized the hanger-on by the tails of his long coaching - coat, and his remonstrances and the figure he made with the placard in one hand and a hammer in the other, and with his mouth full of tacks, as he tried to balance himself on the shoulders of the two Conservatives and snatch

his coat-tails from the wicked Radicals, impressed me very much, though at the time I was
otherwise engaged. Stones and sticks were flying, and fish that were never meant to fly, and
the local inspector of police was begging the
Candidate to go inside and so stop the riot, and
the youngest of both sides were hammering each
other right and left. They continued to throw
things, the women throwing more spitefully than
the men, but not aiming so well, and most of our
party were hit, so that during the rest of our
drive the carriage had a strange odor of a fish-
market.

There were no speeches that night. We all
sat around the house and tried to play cards or
listen to the piano, and talked of everything but
the election on the morrow. The day of the poll
rose clear and calm, but the announcement in
the papers of the morning that the Conservatives
had lost fifteen seats on the day previous did not
send us to B—— rejoicing.

They surround the counting of votes in England with much dignity and a proper degree of
mystery. The votes came into town locked up
in big black tin boxes, carried between two con-
stables of the different villages in the division,
and the boxes were piled in great heaps in the
town-hall. Then those who were to be present
went before a magistrate and swore themselves
to secrecy as to what they were about to see.

About one hundred people took this oath, eighty of whom were the young men who were to do the counting and the officials, and the remainder were a half-dozen friends of each of the candidates.

What I saw, which I am sure my oath of secrecy will allow me to tell, was a long, bare room, with a dozen tables in the centre shut in by a railing. Inside of this railing the young men unfolded and counted out the votes and kept tally. Outside the railing hung the interested ones of both sides—the friends, the late speakers, and the sisters of the rival Candidates. Sometimes the votes at one table would all run one way, and if that was not our way we would crowd along the railing to a table where things were progressing more cheerfully. At each table there were little books with each page marked to hold the record of twenty-five votes, and so by multiplying the number of the page by twenty-five, and adding the result to the results obtained in a similar way at the other tables, one could make a rough guess at how things were going. As a matter of fact, things went entirely too evenly. For one hour, and it seemed much longer than that, we hovered over those rails like gamblers over a roulette-table, or ran to a corner to compare calculations with some one else, the satisfaction of such comparisons being sadly marred by the fact that the Radicals were returning from another corner with cheerful countenances. Some one's arithmetic was most evidently in the wrong.

It was a scene quite different from anything of the sort in this country. We receive the returns here in the seclusion of a private room by wire, and the hated other party can neither hear us swear nor rejoice; but at B—— we had to control our satisfaction when things were coming our way out of deference to our rival's presence, and we dared not show our despair for the same reason. The sisters of the candidates smiled bravely and kept out of each other's company; and the voices of the tellers as they called the names of the candidates monotonously from the twelve tables, and the shuffling of the hurrying feet around the rail, were all that broke the silence of the big room. Outside, beneath the windows, the market-place was packed with a great mob of anxious people, who were almost as silent as those inside.

It was noon before the twisted pieces of paper had sunk from high white piles to a few scattered leaves on the twelve tables. And then one noticed a drawing away of the Radicals from one another, and an equally marked gathering together of the Conservatives, and one heard little gasps of doubt and hope and the louder swaggering tones of congratulation.

The Mayor of B—— rose at last and held the

"THEY RAISED THE CANDIDATE UP"

returns in his hand, and raised his eyes from them
to smile slightly towards My Candidate.. He had
no business to do that, but he was only human.
And then, while he pushed his way towards the
window to officially announce the result of the
poll to the waiting mob, we executed dance steps,
or wrung the Candidate's hand, or punched each
other in the side, or tried to look superior and as
though we had never doubted the result from the
first. But the Radical candidate's sister, who had
driven at his side over so many rainy miles and
sat through so many weary, anxious meetings,
made a straight line for our Candidate's sister,
and held out her hand, and of the two I think she
was the least embarrassed.

"My brother is something of a philosopher,"
she said, bravely; "he will take it well." I was
very glad we had defeated the Radical candidate, but I wished he had left his relatives at
home.

And then we were rushed out into the street,
but not into such an unfriendly mob as that of
the day before. It was all red now, and they were
quite crazy. They raised the Candidate up and
carried him on their shoulders to the stone well
in the market - place, where he made a speech
which no one heard save the reporter, who had
crawled between his legs, because we all yelled
so ; and then we had a luncheon at the inn, and
everybody drank everybody's health, and the

Candidate went to the window every other minute to show himself to the howling crowd and to
bow.   We had meant to return by rail, but that
was much too insipid after such a victory; and
the red postilions appeared suddenly, and the four
white horses, just as the fairy coach did for Cin-
derella, and fourteen other coaches and dog-carts
and drags fell into line behind, and we left B——
at a gallop, all standing up and cheering and waving our flags or hats, and drunk with pleasure and
success.

They telegraphed on ahead that the successful
Candidate was coming, and at each village the
people met us, and unhitched the horses, and
dragged the Candidate's carriage through the
streets, and all the people came to the doors
and hedges and cheered too.   And at every little
thatched cottage the good Conservatives ran into
the road and danced up and down, and at all the
big estates the house-servants and the keepers
and the men from the stables were gathered to
welcome us, just as though they had scented victory from afar; and I regret to say that we stole
most of their flags as we galloped by, and decorated the fourteen carriages, so that it looked like
a trooping of the colors as the cavalcade of union-
jacks went rocking and rising and falling over the
hills.

It was a grand triumphal march of twenty
miles, and the driver beside me lashed his horses

"WERE GATHERED TO WELCOME US"

all the way and muttered to himself without
once stopping, "Sich goings on I never did see.
That I will say; sich goings on I never did see."
It was near six before we reached the big town
near the House, and the people met us three
miles out, on foot and on bicycles and on horseback, and dragged the coach the rest of the way
under rows and rows of swinging flags and between lines of wildly excited people; and the
Member, no longer a Candidate, made a speech
at the Angel Inn—the fifteenth that day—and
the landlord rubbed his hands, and said, cheerfully, "Every window in my 'ouse will be broke
this night," which he accepted as a compliment
to the stanch principles of his inn, which has
been Conservative since the night Charles II.
slept in it. And then we hitched up again, and
rode out of the noisy town and through the
quiet lanes on to the House, more soberly now,
for we were conscious of how much victory
meant there.

The House stands at the end of an avenue of
elms a mile long, and the lodge-keeper had the
great iron gates open in readiness for the first
time in his life, and we raced through. It was
just six, and the sun was going down behind the
House and the great elms, and the park lay half
in shadow and half in twilight, and as we came
swiftly up the homestretch we came so soberly
that the deer did not run away, but merely raised

their heads to look. That door of the House which opens on the mile of elms is one seldom used; it was opened once long ago for William III., and once again more lately for the young prince who died, and again that day for the Member. On the lawn in front of it all the tenants stood in their best clothes, with red wherever they could put it; and on the steps were the ladies from the other houses about, and the officers who had ridden over from the camp, and back of them all the servants in their best livery and powdered hair.

And in the centre, standing very tall and quite alone, with a red silk cloak falling from her shoulders to the stone flagging, was the Lady of the House. And the Member jumped out first and ran up the steps and stooped and kissed her hand, while she did not look at him, but out across the park, because, being a great lady in the land, she could not let these people see how much she cared, as other women could. The Candidate had returned bringing his sheaves with him, and from the steps of the place that had been his home, and to the people who had known him when he was a boy, he made the last speech of his campaign. I do not remember that speech now, except that I went away suddenly in the midst of it, and gazed steadfastly at a somewhat blurred painting of the "Sixth Countess of —— at the age of nine"; but I shall always remember that home-coming—although it was not my home-coming, and although I was a rank outsider and had no business there—and the sun setting behind the gray walls, and the long line of elms throwing their shadows across the park, and the cheering, happy crowd of tenants, and the tall, beautiful figure in the red cloak standing silent and motionless in the centre.

III

UNDERGRADUATE LIFE AT OXFORD

THE Oxford undergraduate impressed me as the most interesting combination of shyness and audacity that I had ever met. His extreme shyness seems to be his chief dissimilarity, not to most Englishmen, but to all other undergraduates. I mistook it at first for hauteur, and a personal disinclination to see more of myself, which, as I had come so many thousand miles to see him, was discouraging in the extreme. But after he had listened to me with marked disapproval for some time he would blush, and ask me to dinner in hall, or mention, as if he were rather ashamed of the fact, that he expected his sisters to tea in his rooms, or that some of the men were coming to breakfast the next morning, and that if I liked I could come too. As he kept this up steadily for the whole of the Eights' week, I decided that he was the most truly hospitable soul I had met in England; most truly so, as social functions of the most simple order were so evidently a trial to him, and the presence of a stranger a cause of much personal embarrassment and distress. But when it was not an occasion of ceremony, and after he had conquered the shyness which at first lay hold upon him, he developed a most reckless and audacious spirit, and I forgot to study him in trying to keep up with his different moves, and to avoid the traps he laid for me, and, owing to being in his company, the wrath of the townsfolk and the clutches of the local constabulary.

The town of Oxford is at its best during the week in which the eight-oared boats of the twenty colleges belonging to the university row for mastery on the river. It is then filled with people up from London. The weather, which is always to be considered first, is the best the year gives, the green quadrangles and the flowers are more beautiful than at any other time, and every afternoon the river overflows with boats. The beauty of Oxford, as everybody knows, does not lie in any one building or in any one street; it is the abundance and continuing nature of its beauty which makes it what it is. It is not like any other show town in that one does not ride or walk from the inn to see a certain cathedral or a particular monument. In Oxford with every step you take you are encompassed and shut in with what is oldest and best in architecture, with what is softest and most beautiful in turf and in window gardens of flowers. You cannot go to the

corner to post a letter without being halted by
some iron gateway which you have not seen before, or a row of mocking gargoyles, or a mysterious coat of arms, or a statue half eaten by the
cannibals of Time and Weather.   You rush
through whole streets — being in a hurry to see
the boats start, or late for a luncheon, or some
such important matter — lined with crumbling
walls or marvellous façades, with glimpses through
great doorways of radiant gardens, or of oaken
halls hung with old paintings and marble tablets.
They are as much a matter of course as are the
fire-escapes in New York, and so common to the
town that you see them as a whole, and regard
them as little as you regard the signs on the
houses as you rush past them on the elevated.
They form part of the very atmosphere, and
those who breathe this atmosphere for any length
of time grow to consider Oxford as a home, and
return to it after many years to find it just as
dear to them and just as beautiful and almost as
old.   I think it is much better to take Oxford
this way than to go over it piece by piece with
Baedeker in hand to acquaint one's self with the
window of the headless scholar, with the tower
that Wolsey built overnight, and the room in
which Dr. Johnson wrote something very important, the name of which I forget.   Personally, I
confess to not knowing the location of more than
three of all the twenty colleges.   They all seemed

to me to run into one another. And then it really did not matter, for you were sure to reach the one for which you had started if you made a sufficient number of wrong turns, and asked your way from every third undergraduate, and disobeyed his directions implicitly. And then the Eights' week is not a time in which one can best linger before stained-glass windows. For the river calls you by day, and there are suppers at night, and the very much alive undergraduates are as worthy of consideration as those who have gone before, and who remain in memorial tablets or on darkened canvas.

Boating is a much more serious business at Oxford than at Yale or Harvard. At either of these two latter universities a 'varsity crew and four class crews are as much as the undergraduates furnish, while at Oxford, where there are no greater number of students, each of the twenty colleges places eight good men in its boat every term, and from them supplies a 'varsity eight as well. And these are only the official representatives of the colleges, for apart from them entirely are the private canoes of many curious makes and many names, besides that noble and worthy institution the Oxford punt. So that every student owns his boat as a matter of course, just as he owns his umbrella, and uses it almost as frequently.

There is a story of a Western Congressman

who asked why the American people should com
plain of the inadequacy of their navy. "All we
want is a few more ships," he said. "We have
water enough." When one sees the Thames at
Oxford and its branch the Cherwell, one is inclined to transpose this, and to admit that the
undergraduates have boats in sufficiency, and
that all they need is a little water. This seems
especially true when a punt strikes your boat in
the stern and two pair of oars form a barrier
above your head, and a confusing chorus of
voices assail you on all sides with "Look ahead,
sir." This, however, adds an element of excitement which would be otherwise lacking, and
teaches you to be polite as well as to row, or
rather to steer, for it can hardly be called rowing
when you back water and unship your oars twice
to every time you take a pull forward. At Oxford a man is first taught how to unship his oars,
and then how to back water. After he can do
this quickly, in spite of the fixed rowlocks, which
custom still fastens to all save the racing-boats,
he is taught the less-used practice of pulling
ahead. But the very number of the boats, while
not conducive to speed, gives the wonderful life
and color to the dark waters and overhanging
trees. The girls in their summer frocks, and the
men in their brilliant blazers and ribboned caps,
and the canoes with colored parasols, make the
little river and its little branch a miniature Hen-

AN OXFORD UNDERGRADUATE

ley or an English Venice, and at the same time
furnish you with an excellent instance of British
conservatism. For no matter how musical or
noisy the men in your boat may be, or how
pretty the women, those in the other boats passing within a yard of you consider you as little as
though you were a part of the bank. Their eyes
avoid you, and their ears as well. A man could
pass between the double rows of punts and canoes tied in the shade to the banks of the Cher-

well, singing or shouting or confessing a murder, or making love to the girl in the bow, and no one of the young men along the bank within reach of his oar would raise his head from his novel, or stop pulling the ears of his ·fox-terrier, or cease considering the bowl of his pipe.

The course over which the races are rowed at Oxford is a little less than a mile. The Thames for that mile is about as wide as an eight-oared boat is long, or ever so little wider, and the last half of the course is lined with house-boats, or "barges," as they call them. Each college has its barge, and each barge is a wonderful thing, colored and carved and gilded and decorated with coats of arms, and with a brilliant flag flapping above it of silk and gold, and as large as a campaign banner. They look like enormous circus band-wagons robbed of their wheels and floated on rafts. The raft part of the barge holds very smart-looking undergraduates in ribboned straw hats and flannels; the barge itself contains a club-room, with racing prints on the walls where there are not windows, a long table for tea, and a dressing-room for the crew. On the top of the barge is a roof-garden of pretty girls, each properly chaperoned to the third and fourth degree; and sometimes, when the college to which the barge belongs thinks it is going to bump the boat of another college, there is a regimental band. Opposite the line of barges, which stretches a quarter of a mile along the bank, is the towing-path, and back of it meadows filled with buttercups and daisies. This towing-path is where those who "run with the boats" follow the race, and where the towns-people gather. There are two races on each day of the Eights' week, one for the ten second-best boats at half-past four, and one at half-past six for the ten first-best boats. So at four o'clock each day the town of Oxford suddenly wakes up, and the people begin to pour out of lodging-houses and quadrangles, and inns and college gardens, and what seems an invading army of young women and their brothers (you can tell they are their brothers because they wear the same ribbons around their hats), march down the High to the river in the middle of the street rather than on the sidewalks, and so increase the similitude to an organized army, and make one wonder how many streets there are at home through which young women in white frocks and young men in pipe-clayed cricket shoes could walk so serenely.

Among these you notice many young men in a sort of undress uniform, which is very undress, but quite uniform. These are the men who run with the boats, and who, to an American, form the most novel and picturesque feature of the races. Each wears a blazer, a cap with his college arms worked upon it, a jersey cut V-shape, a muffler around his neck, heavy knickerbocker

8

stockings turned down at the calf, and a pair of running-breeches, of a *décolleté* nature, which leave his bare knees and most of his legs as free and unimpeded as a Highlander's.

There is no deviation in this costume. It is as rigorous as court dress. No man would think of wearing a high-neck jersey and discarding the heavy muffler, or of leaving off the heavy stockings and substituting long flannel trousers. Men who have run with the boats have always worn just those things. It is a tradition. You can see them in prints and in the illustrations of *Tom Brown at Oxford* and no undergraduate would think of changing it. These men who are going to run continue on up the towpath, the girls mount the different barges, or get into punts or row-boats and block up the river, and the sedate undergraduates distribute themselves about on the raft part of whichever barge is called for by the ribbon on their hats. It is quite impossible not to come back to these ribbons. No one knows until he goes to Oxford how many combinations can be made out of the primary colors; there are almost as many as there are combinations in a pack of cards. Each college has its ribbon, and each college crew, cricket and football team, and all of its various dining or debating societies, have their individual ribbon, and no two are alike. As there are twenty colleges, this calls for many varieties of ribbon. Those men

who are on the 'varsity Elevens or Eights wear
a broad, dark-blue ribbon, which gives them the
proud title of " a Blue." You say a man has got
his Blue as you say Lord Rosebery has been given
the Garter, or you say a man is a Blue just as you
say such a one is an M.P. or a V.C., only you say
it with more awe. When I first went to Oxford
the shopkeeper offered me my choice of three
hundred combinations of colors for my hat, and
I proposed in my ignorance, and in order to avoid
any possible assumption of membership, to deco-
rate it with one of plain, modest dark blue. If I
had asked the yeoman of the guard to deck me
out in the regalia in the Tower of London, I could
not have been crushed with a more indignant
scorn or a more abrupt refusal. One man was
pointed out to me at Oxford over half a dozen
times as " So - and - so of Pembroke." This was
all I was ever told; I was evidently supposed
to know the rest; but as I did not, I asked one
day, expecting to hear he was a Senior Wrang-
ler, or a Newdigate prize, or the Son of Somebody, which latter does not count for much at
Oxford; but I was told that he was the only
man in the university who had made a serious
study of the college ribbons; that this was his
life's work, his particular *métier*, and I learned to
bow with respect to the one man who can distin-
guish by a glance at five hundred passing undergraduates those who belong to the Palmerston

Club and those who play on the eleven for Magdalen.

A bumping race seems a most inexplicable and
rather absurd affair to Americans as they hear
of it, but it impresses you, if you see it often
enough, as an institution of distinctly sporting
qualities. It is a triumph of mind over matter,
the matter in this particular being the banks of
the Thames, which lie so close together at Oxford that it is not possible for two boats to row
abreast for any great distance. To overcome
this, the undergraduates of long ago invented
the bumping race. Its principle is briefly this:
A certain number of boats are placed, one after
the other, in a line at equal distances apart ; they
are then started at the same instant, and the object of each boat is to increase the distance between itself and the boat immediately behind it,
and to bump with its bow the stern of the boat
immediately in front. There are two races a day
for one week, and the boats that are bumped on
the first day drop back on the next day, and
start one place lower down in the line—that is,
if the fourth boat of the ten which start bumps
number three, number three on the next day will
drop to fourth place, and number four will proudly move up higher, and try to bump number
two.

There is really no regular finish, so far as the
spectator is concerned, to a bumping race, be-

cause a bump may take place anywhere along the course, and one is just as likely to see the best of the race at one point on the bank as at another. But the barges line the upper end of the river, where all those boats still unbumped stop after they have reached a certain point. The start is made quite out of sight of the barges a mile down the river, at the upper end of one of its sharpest turns.

To see and appreciate a bumping race proper-ly, you should watch the start of one race, the finish of another, and at another time "run with the boats" along the bank. The boats leave the several barges to take up their places at the start in an inverse order to that in which they return —that is, the boat which is to tail the procession coming back will row over the course first, and so avoid the necessity of having another boat crowd past it. As the first eight men start off, the sedate undergraduates stamp their walking-sticks into the flooring, and express their satis-faction at the sight by guttural murmurs of approval of a most well-bred and self-contained nature ; and the rival crews, who are drawn up in their boats beside the other barges, lift their oars slightly and rattle them in the rowlocks as a sa-lute. Then the men of the first eight pull off their sweaters and throw them to the undergrad-uates on the floating raft, and the trainer takes the blade of the stroke's oar and shoves them

out into the stream; and the cockswain, who is
always a most noisy and excitable little bully,
who abuses and beseeches his crew, and shows
not the least gratitude to them for giving him
such a pleasant and rapid row, cries " Get away !"
angrily, and the eight bend nicely together, and
on the third stroke are well off, with a special attention to form for the benefit of the spectators
on the barges.   There is just room for them to
turn when they reach the starting - place below
the bend, which is in front of hanging willows
and broad low meadows and an old inn.   On one
side lies the towing-path, a narrow, dusty road
close to the bank, and on the other the green
fields.   At regular intervals along the towing-
path wooden posts mark the station of the ten
competing boats, which are kept in place by a
waterman, who holds the bow with a boat-hook,
and by the cockswain, who further steadies the
boat by holding one end of a cord, the other
end of which is fastened to the bank, while he
clutches the tiller-ropes in his right.   There are
two signal - guns — one five minutes before the
start, and the second four minutes later.   At the
first gun each of the ten boats, lying a hundred
feet apart, moves out into the stream, the waterman of each pushing the bow from the bank, the
cockswain leaning forward and meeting the tug-
ging of the oars with the backward pressure of
the cord; and the time - keepers, of which each

boat has one, count aloud the last minute. If it is a still afternoon, you can hear the nearest of them counting together, the men in the boats sitting meanwhile as immovable as figure-heads on a man-of-war, and the five or six hundred bare-kneed runners on the towpath, who are waiting to race with their own boat, to encourage or warn her crew as the need may be, standing counting also, but silently and with only their lips moving.

" Thirty seconds gone," count the time - keepers; " forty seconds gone; fifty seconds gone. Four—three—two—one—row," and at the last word the ten cockswains shout in unison, the eighty broad backs lunge forward, and the scramble to touch the boat ahead and to keep out of the clutches of the one behind begins, and continues for six feverish minutes. There is one advantage about a bumping race in that the men can see how near they are to being bumped, while they cannot see without turning completely in their seats how near they are to bumping the boat in front. The advantage of this lies in the fact that they are always sure to pull their best when the danger is greatest, and that the cockswain can make them believe they are gaining on the boat in front by simply saying so. To further warn them and to guide the cockswain, who cannot look behind him, three men accompany each boat along the bank with

a bell and a revolver and a policeman's rattle.
The sounding of any of these signifies the distance one boat is from the other.

It is a very different scene at the other end of
the course. The green meadows there are crowded with people, and the floating grand-stands of
barges, each with its flag, like a company of soldiers, stand as in review for the march past. For
a time hundreds of little boats move along the
bank and block the channel or cling to the rafts
of the barges, and the punts of the Thames con-
servancy scurry from side to side with belated
undergraduates and towns-people. And then the
river grows very still, and every one listens. A
gun from very far off sends a report lazily across
the meadows, and half the people say, " It's the
first," and the other half that it is the " second,"
and while they are discussing this the gun sounds
again, and every one says, " One minute more."
It is quite still now, strangely so to an American accustomed to college yells ringing at an
athletic meeting even before the contestants
have left the hotels for the grounds. And he
misses the rah-rahs and the skyrocket cries and
the inquiries as to who's all right, and the songs
in which the fame and name of some college
hero is being handed down to his four years of
immortality. He compares the rival cries of the
different observation cars along the New Haven
course with this polite and easy patience. It

ON THE CHERWELL

might be a garden-party or a sailing race for all
the enthusiasm there is in advance.   The birds
in the meadows chirp leisurely, the calm of a
bank holiday in London settles on the crowd,
and the river nods and rocks the boats gently as
though it meant to put them to sleep, and then
from very far off you think you hear a faint
clamor of men's voices, but it dies out so suddenly that before you can say, "They're off,"
you are glad you did not commit yourself, and
then it comes again, and now there is no doubt
about it.   It is like the roar of the mob in a
play, unformed and uneven, and growing slowly
sharper and fiercer, but still like a roar, and not
measured and timed as the cheering is at home.
There is something quite stern and creepy about
it, this volume of angry sounds breaking in on
the quiet of such a sunny afternoon, and then
you see the first advance - guard of the army
which is making the uproar, and the prow of the
first boat with the water showing white in front,
and the eight broad backs lunging and bending
back and forth and shooting up and down the
limit of the sliding-seat as they dart around the
turn.   You have seen men row before, but it is
quite safe to say you have never seen anything
like that which is coming towards you along the
broad towpath.   If you have ever gone to an
athletic meeting you may possibly have seen as
many as twenty men start together in a quarter-

mile handicap race with the whole field grouped
within six yards of the line, and you may have
thought it pretty as they all got off together in a
bunch. But imagine, not twenty men within six
yards of one another, but hundreds stretching
shoulder to shoulder for half a mile along a
winding road, all plunging and leaping and pushing and shoving, and shouting with the full
strength of their voices, slipping down the bank
and springing up again, stopping to shout at
some particular man until others, not so particular, push them out of their path, and others
tear on and leave them struggling in the rear
and falling farther and farther behind their boat.
Five hundred men, each in a different color, blue
and bright scarlet, striped or spotted, parsons in
high waistcoats and flannel trousers, elderly dons
with children at home, in knickerbockers, and
hundreds of the uniformed barelegged runners
shooting their pistols and ringing the bells, and
all crying and shouting at once: "Magdalen!
Magdalen! well rowed, Magdalen! Pembroke!
you have them, Pembroke! Balliol! well rowed,
Balliol!" When the last boat has passed, the
others not in the race sweep out over the river
and bridge it from bank to bank, and the dusty
runners on the towpath throw up their heels
and dive into the stream, and cross it with six
short strokes, and scramble up on their barge
and shake themselves like Newfoundland dogs,

causing infinite concern for their safety to their sisters, and stampeding the smartly dressed undergraduates in alarm. And then every one goes into the barge and takes tea, for, on the whole, but for the turbulent five hundred, a bumping race is conducted with infinite discretion and outward calm.

The Oxford undergraduate lives in an atmosphere of tradition, and his life is encompassed with rules which the American undergraduate would find impossible, but which impress the visitor as both delightful and amusing. It is an amusing rule, for instance, which forbids the undergraduate to smoke after ten o'clock under penalty of a fine, which fine is increased by twopence if the smoking is continued after eleven o'clock. There is something so delightfully inconsequential in making smoking more pernicious at eleven than at ten. And the rule which fines an undergraduate of Balliol and his friends as well if he or they pass the gate after nine: I used to leave that college for no other reason than to hear the man at the gate say, "You are charged to Mr. ——, sir," which meant that one of the undergraduates would have to pay the college one large penny because I chose to go out and come in again at the unnatural hour of ten in the evening. There were also some delightful rules as to when and where the undergraduate must appear in his cap and gown, which latter he wears with a careless contempt that would greatly shock the Seniors of the colleges in the Western States who adopt the hat and gown annually, and announce the fact in the papers. It struck me as a most *décolleté* garment, and was in most cases very ragged, and worn without much dignity, for it only hung from the shoulders to the waist like a knapsack, or was carried wrapped up in a bundle in one hand.

The day of an Oxford man is somewhat different from that of an American student. He rises at eight, and goes to chapel, and from chapel to breakfast in his own room, where he gets a most substantial breakfast—I never saw such substantial breakfasts anywhere else — or, what is more likely, he breakfasts with some one else in some one else's rooms. This is a most excellent and hospitable habit, and prevails generally. So far as I could see, no one ever lunched or dined or breakfasted alone. He either was engaged somewhere else or was giving a party of his own. And it frequently happened that after we were all seated our host would remember that he should be lunching with another man, and we would all march over to the other man's rooms and be received as a matter of course. It was as if they dreaded being left alone with their thoughts. It struck me as a university for the cultivation of hospitality before anything else.

After breakfast the undergraduate "reads" a

bit, and then lunches with another man, and reads a little more, and then goes out on the river or to the cricket-field until dinner. The weather permits this out-of-door life all the year round, which is a blessing the Oxford man enjoys and which his snow-bound American cousin does not. His dinner is at seven, and if in hall it is a very picturesque meal. The big hall is rich with stained glass and full-length portraits of celebrated men whose names the students never by any possible chance know, and there are wooden carved wainscotings and heavy rafters. There is a platform at one end on which sit the dons, and below at deal tables are the undergraduates in their gowns—worn decorously on both shoulders now, and not swinging from only one—and at one corner by themselves the men who are training for the races. The twilight is so late that the place needs only candles, and there is a great rattle of silver mugs that bear the college arms, and clatter of tongues, and you have your choice of the college ale or the toast and water of which you used to read and at which you probably wondered in *Tom Brown at Oxford*. The dons are the first to leave, and file out in a solemn procession. If you dine with the dons and sit above your fellow-men you are given the same excellent and solid dinner and wine in place of beer, and your friends of the morning make faces at you for deserting them and because of your higher estate.

My first dinner with the dons was somewhat confusing. After a most excellent service some-body rose, and I started with the rest down the steps towards the door, when my host stopped me and said, "You have forgotten to bring your napkin." What solemn rite this foretold I could not guess. I had enjoyed my dinner, and I wanted to smoke, and why I needed a napkin, unless as a souvenir, I could not see; and I con-tinued wondering as we marched in some certain order of precedence up and down stone stair-ways and through gloomy passages to another room in an entirely different part of the college, where we found another long table spread as carefully as the one in the hall below with many different wines and fruits and sweets. And we all sat down at this table as before, and sipped port and passed things around and talked learn-edly, as dons should, for half an hour, when we rose, and I again bade my host good-night, but he again stopped me with a deprecatory smile, and again we formed a procession and marched solemnly through passages and over stone floors to another room, where a third table was spread, with more bottles, coffee, and things to smoke. It struck me that an Oxford don mixes some high living with his high thinking. I did not wait to see if there were any more tables hidden around the building, but I suppose there were.

After dinner the undergraduate reads with his

tutor out of college or in his own rooms. He
cannot leave the college after a certain early
hour, and if he should stay out all night the con-
sequences would be awful. This is, of course,
quite as incomprehensible to an American as are
the jagged iron spikes and broken glass which
top the college walls. It seems a sorry way to
treat the sons of gentlemen, and more fitted to
the wants of a reformatory. There is one gate
at Trinity which is only open for royalty, and
which was considered to be insurmountable by
even the most venturesome undergraduate, until
one youth scaled it successfully, only to be caught
out of bounds. The college authorities had no
choice in the matter but to send him down, as
they call suspending a man in Oxford; but so
great was their curiosity and belief in the virtue
of the gate that they agreed to limit his term of
punishment if he would show them how he scaled
it. To this, of course, he naturally agreed, and the
undergraduates were edified by the sight of one
of their number performing a gymnastic feat of
rare daring on the top of the sacred iron gate,
while the college dignitaries stood gazing at him
in breathless admiration from below.

Another undergraduate of another college was
caught out of bounds one night by the proctor,
but promised a merely nominal punishment if he
would disclose by what means he escaped, for the
walls surrounding the college were deemed im-

pregnable. He had to choose between taking a heavy sentence and leaving the means of escape still a secret, or sacrificing his companions and shutting off all their further excursions by saving himself. He asked the authorities to allow him three days' time in which he might decide whether he would or would not tell. This was granted him, with the warning that if he did not tell he would be sent down. At the end of the three days he appeared before the college board and said he had decided to tell them how he had escaped. "You will find my answer," he said, "in the eighteenth Psalm, twenty-ninth verse," and then left the room. The dignitaries hurriedly opened a prayer-book, and found the following: "By the help of my God have I leaped over the wall." The young man was not sent down nor the leak in the wall closed. I fear, from all I could hear, that almost every college prison in Oxford has its secret exit and entrance, known only to the undergraduates. Sometimes it is a coal-hole, and sometimes a tree which stretches a friendly branch over the spiked wall, and sometimes a sloping roof and a drop of eight feet to the pavement; but there is always something. No lock ever was invented that could not be picked. The pity is that there should be a lock at all. It is only fair to say of these prisons that they are the loveliest prisons in the world, and that they are only prisons by night. By day the

HOW SOME WEAR THE GOWN

gardens and lawns of the quadrangles, as cultivated and old and beautiful as any in England, are
as free, and one wonders how any one ever studies
there.   One generally associates study with the
green-baize table, a student-lamp, a wet towel, and
a locked door.   How men can study looking out
on turf as soft and glossy as green velvet, with
great gray buttresses and towers about it, and
with rows above rows of window boxes of flowers
set into the gray walls like orchids on a dead
tree, and a lawn-tennis match going on in one
corner, is more than I can understand.   The only
obvious answer is that they do not study.   I am
sure the men I knew did not.   But there must
be some who do, else from where would come
the supply of dons?

Different colleges turn out different classes of
men.   The reading men, who go in for firsts and
scholarships and such distinctions, haunt one college; the fast set, who wear the blue and white
ribbon of the Bullingdon Club, go to another;
the conservative, smart, and titled men go to a
third; the nobodies flock by themselves; and the
athletes foregather somewhere else, and so help
to make up the personality of the whole university.

If I were asked to pick out the characteristic
of the Oxford undergraduate which struck me as
being conspicuous as his occasional shyness, I
would say it was his love of "ragging," and that

when he is indulging in what he calls a "rag," at some one else's expense, he is in his most interesting and picturesque mood.

A rag is a practical joke. It may be a simple rag, and consist of nothing more harmful than mild chaffing, or it may be an ornate and carefully prepared and rehearsed rag, involving numerous accomplices and much ingenuity and daring. It is in the audacity of these latter, and in the earnestness in which they are carried out, that the Oxford undergraduate differs most widely from the undergraduate of America. The Yale or Harvard Sophomore does a wild thing occasionally, but he does it, I fear, chiefly to tell about it later, and is rather relieved when it is over. He points with pride to the barber-poles in his study, but he does not relish the half-hour's labor and danger spent in capturing them. The Oxford man, on the contrary, enjoys mischief for mischief's sake; he will never boast of it later, and he will leave one evil act and turn abruptly to another if it appears to offer more attractive possibilities of entertainment. And he carries off his practical joking or chaffing with a much more easy and audacious air. This, I think, is due to class feeling, which is in the atmosphere in England, and which does not exist with us. The Harvard student may think he is of finer clay than the towns-people and the tradesman and policeman, as he generally is, but he cannot bring *them* to think so too. That is where his English contemporary has so much the advantage of him. The Oxford townsman feels an inborn and traditional respect for the gentleman; he bows meekly to his eccentricities; he takes his chaff with smiles, and regards the undergraduate's impertinences as one of the privileges of the upper classes. And the Oxford man knows it, and imposes on him accordingly.

It is rather difficult to give instances of a rag and avoid making the undergraduate appear anything but absurd. One cannot show in writing the earnestness and seriousness with which these practical jokes are conducted, nor the business-like spirit in which they are carried out. Without this they lose the element of audacity which always saves them from being absurd, and raises them to the plane of other flights of the imagination ably performed. The men I knew seemed to live in an element of mischief. They would keep me talking with flattering interest until the clock struck twelve, when they would leap to their feet and explain that it was now past the hour when any one could leave the college, and that my only means of exit would have to be either down to the pavement by a rope of sheets, or up through it by means of the coal-hole.

Everything they saw suggested a rag, as everything in the pantomime is material for mischief for the clown in the pantaloon. A mail-coach standing in front of a public-house deserted by its driver furnished them with the means of conveyance into the country, where they abandoned her Majesty's mail-wagon three miles out of town, with the horse grazing by the hedges. A hand-organ suggested their disguising themselves as Italians and playing the organ around Oxford, which they did to the satisfaction of the populace and themselves, their expenses being three pounds and their returns two shillings, one of which was given them by a friend who did not recognize them, and who begged them to move on.

One night during Eights' week a group of men stopped to speak to a friend who was permitted to room outside of the college. It was a very warm, close night in June, and he came to the door dressed only in his bath robe. "I will make you," one of the men said, "a sporting proposition. I will bet you five shillings that you won't run to the corner and back in your bath robe." He said that if they would make it ten shillings he would run the distance and leave the bath robe in their hands. They accepted this amendment, and after he had fairly started went inside his house with the bath robe and locked the front door. The impudence of Powers in *Charles O'Malley* was equalled by one man who said while showing some ladies around the quadrangle of Balliol, "That is the Master's dining-room, that on the floor above is the Master's study window, and that," he added, picking up a stone from the gravel walk and hurling it through the window, "is the Master himself." On another night during Eights' week three of them disguised themselves as a proctor and two of his bull-dogs, and captured a visiting friend of mine from America, who had been led into their hands by myself and others in the plot, and then basely deserted. The mock proctor and his men declared the American was Lord Encombe, of Magdalen, and fined him ten shillings for being out of college after hours without his cap and gown. He protested that he had no connection with the university, but they were quite as positive that they knew him very well, and gave him his choice of paying the fine or going instantly to jail, and as he had a very vague idea of British law and the university regulations he gave them the money. This they later returned to him with his card before as many of the college as we could gather together, to his intense disgust. He is now waiting with anxious hospitality for the first Oxford undergraduate who visits America, and promises that that unfortunate individual will not return home before he has been brought before every police justice in New York.

The most conspicuous and most generally known instance of ragging is, of course, the way the undergraduates conduct the exercises during

Commemoration week. I confess I looked forward to this with wicked anticipation. I had read of it, and had heard those who had seen it tell of it, and I questioned if it were so bad as it was painted, even though I had seen to what lengths the undergraduate would go.

The Sheldonian Theatre is a single circular building, formed inside like a clinic-room in a hospital, but decorated grandly inside and out, and open to the sunlight by great windows. It is topped by a magnificent dome. In the morning of the day when the degrees were to be bestowed it was filled from the floor up to this dome with young girls and their chaperons in the lightest and brightest and most brilliant of summer frocks. They rose tier upon tier in unbroken circles to the balcony, where they began again, and ranged on up to the very top. It was a very pretty sight, for the sun shone in through the stained windows in broad, generous rays, and the lesser authorities of the university, who acted as ushers, wore their red silk hoods and gowns, and moved in and out among the women, looking very learned and fine as the sun touched their white hair and their long mantles of rustling silk. Standing on the floor in the circle formed by the lower balcony were the visitors and the college dons in black robes, or in the blue serge of every day. There were no seats for them, and so they moved about like bears in a bear-pit, gaz-

ing up at their friends, and pointing out the celebrities, and talking familiarly of the great men
who were about to be honored. A great organ
on one side rumbled out soft and not too difficult music (at home we would have spoiled it
with a brass band) and helped to make the whole
scene impressive and dignified and beautiful.

But as I had come to hear the undergraduates
misbehave, I was disappointed, and so expressed
myself. The man who had brought me pointed
to the balcony, and showed where different
groups of students were sitting together, looking
very good and keeping very quiet among severe
matrons and fresh, sweet-looking girls. I recognized several of my friends among the students.
They appeared gloomy and resigned. Some one
explained this by saying that the women had
been crowded into the balcony to scatter the
groups of undergraduates and to shame them
into silence. I was exceedingly disappointed.
There were three young men leaning over the
balcony facing the organist, a Mr. Lopes. He
was playing something of Chopin's gently, as
though he did not want to interfere with the
talk, and the dons and the girls in the circles
were whispering, as though they did not want to
interrupt the music. It was a pretty, well-bred
scene, a mixture of academic dignity with a
touch of the smartness of the town. And so we
waited politely for the procession of dignitaries

to appear.   And as we waited, whispering, there
came suddenly on the hushed warm summer air
a boy's voice, not rudely or " freshly," but with
the quiet, authoritative drawl of an English gentleman.

" Mr. Lopes," said the voice, and the whispering ceased with a start, and the organist's fingers
hesitated on the keys.—" Mr. Lopes, I do not
care much for Chopin myself. Can you play
' Ta-ra-ra boom de-ay ' ?"

From the other side of the gallery a young
man sprang excitedly to his feet. " Oh no, sir,
don't play that !" he cried, eagerly. " Play the
' Old Kent Road.'   *I* can sing that."

" I've heard him sing it," a third voice joined
in, anxiously, " and I hope, sir, you will play
almost anything else."

That was the beginning.   From that on for
one hour the building was absolutely at the
mercy of the undergraduates.   Then one of the
three men who were leaning over the balcony,
and as plainly in view as actors on a stage, proposed three cheers for the ladies.   The response
to this showed that though the undergraduates
were broken up into small bodies they were as
one grand unit in their desire to take a prominent part in the exercises.

" And let me ask," added the young man who
had proposed the cheers, politely, " that you give
one more cheer for the two young ladies in pink

DOING A BIT OF READING

just coming in, and who, though rather late, are, nevertheless, very welcome."

This speech, which was accompanied with a polite bow, and followed by enthusiastic cheers, turned the two young ladies into the color of their frocks, and drove them back terrified into the quadrangle. The men who made all the trouble did not attempt to hide in the crowd about them, or to address the public anonymously. They were, on the contrary, far from shrinking from view, and apparently just as far from imagining that any one would consider they were the least forward. Their manner was serious, and rather that of a public censor who was more bored than otherwise by his duties, but who was determined that the proceedings should go off with dignity.

"Come, sir," they would say, very shortly, " you really must attend to your duties. You have been conversing with the lady in the blue bonnet for the last five minutes, and several ladies are waiting to be shown their places."

They did not laugh at their own impertinences, or in any way act as if they thought they were doing anything amusing or peculiar. It was the earnestness of their manner and their mock anxiety that all should go right which made it funny. And the most absurd thing about it was the obvious awe and terror in which the authorities stood of them. But the

audience of severe matrons and learned dons
and timid, shy girls gazed stolidly before them,
and took the most audacious piece of insolence
in that same unmoved calm with which they
listened to the Greek oration.

The Vice - Chancellor entered at the head of a
grand procession of beadles with gold maces, followed by those who were to receive degrees, and
plunged with a very red face and nervous manner into his Latin address, through which he
raced breathlessly, with his nose glued to the
page and his ears deaf to interruptions. They
began by telling him, " Don't be shy, sir," and
" Speak louder, sir ;" and then one man suggested doubtfully that it was " rather too good to
be original ;" and another said, warningly, " You
had better be careful, sir ; you cribbed that line."
Another laughed indulgently, and said, in a con-
fidential tone of encouragement : " Don't mind
them, sir. *I'll* listen to you ;" and another, after
a pause, exclaimed, with a little sigh of satisfaction, " Now, you know, *I* call it rather good."
The unfortunate Vice-Chancellor blushed redder
than before at this, and in turning over a page
hesitated at the word "ut." " Ut," he repeated.
In an instant twenty men had thrown themselves anxiously across the balcony. " Be careful, sir," they cried, in agony, " be careful. Do
not forget the subjunctive."

" Ah," they added, with a sigh of relief, " he

knew; he knew;" and to this a sceptic added, gloomily: " I don't believe he knew. Some one must have prompted him." Then another voice said, reprovingly, " I trust, sir, you do not intend to take up our time much longer," and the Vice-Chancellor dropped back into his throne, and, with the perspiration rolling down his face, folded his robes about him and smiled delightedly at every other attack on every one else during the exercises.

I suppose no such scene is reproduced in any other country. It is almost impossible to believe that such a situation exists out of one of Mr. Gilbert's operas. The head of the greatest university of the world, surrounded by all the men of it and other universities, and those men highest in art or literature or statesmanship, and each of them in turn at the mercy of a hundred boys not yet of age, literally trembling before them, and finding the honor to which they have looked forward turned into a penance and a nightmare. One undergraduate explained it partly by saying that there were some men who came to Oxford to receive degrees who thought they were conferring rather than receiving honor, and it is for their especial benefit that the ragging is intended. " It puts them in their place," as one boy said, gravely. " They may be big men up in London, but it is just as well they should know we don't think so much of them here."

10

The big men who received degrees on the day I was present were treated rather mildly. All but a very fat professor from Dublin University, who was hailed as "the best Dublin Stout," and an Indian Prince who appeared in cloth of gold and covered with stars and orders. He had a somewhat dusky countenance, and one of the voices asked, anxiously, "Now, sir, *have* you used Pears' soap?" which called forth a chorus of "Shame!" and the foreign prince was loudly cheered to make up for the only remark of the morning which struck one as being ungentle-manly.

IV

LONDON IN THE SEASON

ONDON always impresses one at any time, in season or out of season, as such a great show city, a show city where all classes of people may find entertainment in the life of the city itself—an entertainment which is not dependent on a pretty taste in architecture, or a knowledge of the city's historical values, or even upon a familiarity with its language. It presents so many and such dissimilar points of view that the Frenchman who objects to its sombreness will find something else to take the place of the lightness and gayety of his own capital, as the African monarch who visited London last summer found his greatest delight not in the majesty of its great extent, but in the "blue kings," as he called those who stood at the meeting of the highways, and who, by a mere raising of the hand, directed the flow of traffic, and stopped even him until an omnibus passed by.

And the show is so free. There is so much
which comes to one for nothing, which is given
without the payment of a shilling fee, and which
requires no guide-book. An idle man can find
entertainment from early morn until midnight,
though not later than that, at no greater cost
than the mere exercise of living and standing
on one side to watch. He does not necessarily
have to hunt for the interesting things. They
will come to him *en route*. There is nothing
so picturesque in any other city of the world,
perhaps, or which gives you such a start of curious pleasure, as the Bluecoat boy swinging
along the crowded street, as unconscious of his
yellow legs and flapping skirts and of the rain
beating on his bare head as is the letter-carrier
at home of his mail-bag. Or the Lord Mayor's
carriage blocks your way when you go into the
City to draw on your letter of credit; or a
couple of young barristers in waving gowns and
with wigs askew dash in front of your hansom;
or you are stopped by a regiment of soldiers,
or a group of negro minstrels dancing in the
street with as little concern as though they were
separated from you by a row of foot-lights; or
you meet the Despatch and the other coaches
coming along Piccadilly and going down the
steep hill from that street to St. James's Palace
on a trot, and at the risk of every one's neck,
apparently; or the Lifeguards go by with shin-

ing helmets, and with the lonely rear-guard two hundred yards behind the rest to prevent an unexpected attack from that quarter, from whom I never could guess; or you come suddenly upon the proud and haughty Piccadilly goat in its rambles, or a line of sandwich-men dressed like sailors or cooks; or you note the contrast between the victoria with the men on the box in pink silk stockings and powdered hair, and the little coster's cart piled high with cabbages—as incongruous a sight to any other city as would be a yoke of oxen on Fifth Avenue.

But what make the streets of London most interesting are not the badges of office and official uniforms, but the unofficial garb and insignia which the masses have adopted — the milkman's white apron and wooden yoke, the commissionnaire's medals which tell of campaigns in Egypt and India, or the bootblack's red coat. In America we hate uniforms because they have been twisted into meaning badges of servitude; our housemaids will not wear caps, nor will our coachmen shave their mustaches. This tends to make every class of citizen look more or less alike. But in London you can always tell a 'bus-driver from the driver of a four-wheeler, whether he is on his box or not. The Englishman recognizes that if he is in a certain social grade he is likely to remain there, and so, instead of trying to dress like some one else in a class to which he will never reach, he "makes up" for the part in life he is meant to play, and the 'bus-driver buys a high white hat, and the barmaid is content to wear a turned-down collar and turned-back cuffs, and the private coachman would as soon think of wearing a false nose as a mustache. He accepts his position and is proud of it, and the butcher's boy sits up in his cart just as smartly, and squares his elbows and straightens his legs and balances his whip with as much pride, as any driver of a mail-cart in the Park.

All this helps to give every man you meet an individuality. The hansom-cab driver is not ashamed of being a hansom-cab driver, nor is he thinking of the day when he will be a boss contractor and tear up the streets over which he now crawls looking for a fare, and so he buys artificial flowers for himself and his horse, and soaps his rubber mat, and sits up straight and business-like, and if you put him into livery you would not have to teach him how to look well in it. He does not, as do our own drivers, hang one leg over the edge of his seat, or drive with one leg crossed over the other and leaning forward with shoulders stooped as though he were fishing with his whip. The fact that you are just as good as the next man, as the Constitution says you are, does not absolve you for performing the very humble work you chance to

be doing, in spite of the Constitution, in a slov-
enly spirit.

The first show of the day in London is the procession of horses in the Row. It lasts from nine
to eleven. It used to take place in the afternoon,
but fashion has changed that; and Englishmen
who have been in the colonies, and who come
home on leave, and walk out to the Row at four
to see the riders, seldom find more than a dozen
from which to pick and choose; and they will
find even a greater difference, if they go at the
right hour, in the modern garb of both the men
and the women. At least it was so last summer.
The light habit and high hat of the girls and the
long trousers and cutaway coat of the men had
given way to a dishabille just as different as dress
can be, and just as rigorous in its dishabille as in
its previous correctness and "form." The women
who rode last summer wore loose belted blouses
and looser coats that fell to their knees, straw
hats, and their hair, instead of being bound tight-
ly up, was loose and untidy, and the men appeared in yellow boots, or even leggings, and
serge suits and pot-hats. All these things were
possible because the hour was early, and because
women who follow the hounds dress more with
an eye to comfort than they did, and others dress
like them to give the idea that they too follow
the hounds.

The Row, with six hundred horses on it, is one

of the finest sights of this show city. It would not be possible were it not for the great leisure class, and it and all the other features of Hyde Park show not only how the leisure class is recognized as an institution in the way the authorities have set aside places for it, but how the people themselves not of that class bow to it, and give it the right of way. There is nothing so curious or incomprehensible to an American as this tacit recognition that somebody is better than somebody else. We never could get any one to admit that in this country—except those who thought they were the better ones, and they are so many!

After you have seen the Row, you can walk down to St. James's Palace and watch them change the guard. This is a very innocent recreation, but it is a pretty sight, and it illustrates what I am trying to show—that there is so much to see in London that is done simply because it is decorative and pretty to look at; that it is a thing we do not, I think, sufficiently consider. We do things, first, because they are necessary or convenient, or because they save time; and later, very much later, we make them look presentable. Any one who saw the trees in Madison Square hung with colored lanterns on the occasion of the Columbian celebration in New York must have been struck with this. The awe of the people who walked through that very beautiful park that

THE ROW—MORNING

night, and their bewilderment at having something given them for nothing, which had no use, which was merely ornamental, was rather pathetic. They could have understood the lighting of the city by electricity in place of gas, but not the hanging of orange globes in the green branches of a public square. But the English go about this differently; they still light their streets by gas, but they take a band of music to do as simple a thing as changing a guard. We have no guards in America, not even around the White House, but if we had, we would relieve it at a quickstep and in a most business-like manner.

But in London the band plays every day at a quarter to eleven, and a great crowd of people gathers, and the soldiers and the crowd listen to three selections from the band, and then the men salute the flag, and march off proudly to a swinging march; and the crowd breaks up and goes off about its business, and there is no great harm done; and there has been, on the contrary, some very good music and a brave showing of red coats, which helps the recruiting sergeants.

If you hurry from St. James's Palace yard to Trafalgar Square, you will be in time to see the coaches start from in front of the Hotel Victoria. That is also a pretty sight, and as there are seldom less than a dozen coaches, and as there are a great many passengers to mount, and cold Scotches to be taken, and extra pulls to be given to the harness, it takes some time.   If you make a habit of going down to see the coaches start, you will soon notice that there are many more who do the same thing, and you will see the same gentlemen gather there every morning in very long coats and very curly hats, who examine the same legs of the same horses, and comment on Mr. King's being behind time, or on the fact that Arthur Fownes is not going to drive, or on some such other important matter.   There is a great deal of color and cheery ringing blasts of the horns, and jangling of chains, and old-time picturesqueness in the red-and-green coats of the guards and the familiar names on the panels, and it is rather interesting to note that it is owing to the delight which the visiting American takes in this out-of-town travel that the coaches are able to start with all the places taken.

Of course the best of all the free shows in London are the Houses of Parliament.   They are more interesting to an American than our Upper and Lower House are to an Englishman, because the American knows more about what he is going to see than does the Englishman, and because he, having read history and the foreign column of his daily paper, enjoys that rare pleasure of finding things just as he has been told he would find them, and knows what is going on.   He speaks the language, as it were, and knows his way about, and does not have to keep his nose in the libretto, and so miss all the acting. I once met an Englishman I knew at a club in America which happened to be crowded with famous men, and told him he was very fortunate in seeing so many distinguished Americans gathered in one place and at one time, and I began pointing them out. But as he had never heard of any of them, he saw nothing but a number of elderly gentlemen in evening dress, and did not benefit by his opportunity; so I took him on to an athletic club, where he shot at a mark, and apparently enjoyed himself very much. An American of the same class would have read the books or the speeches of the men pointed out, and could have talked to them, if he had met them, with benefit to both.

This is a characteristic of the American which our English cousin misunderstands in a most aggravating fashion. He explains the fact that we know more about his country and its laws and great men than he does about ours as a perfectly natural tribute to its superiority, just as the Western man is expected to know who is Governor of New York State, while the inhabitant of New York is excused if he does not recollect who may be Governor of Idaho or Dakota. This is not the proper view at all. The American knows more about England than Englishmen know about America because he is interested in the world at large, and not only in the county or borough in which he exists. He would feel ashamed if he did not know. The Englishman is not ashamed. He thinks it perfectly natural that you should recognize all the principal men of both benches in the House of Commons, but he does not feel that he has missed anything, or that there is anything missing in him, when he sees nothing in the House of Representatives but a large room filled with men of whom he has never heard. A member of the cabinet of last June asked me whether our cabinet ministers did or did not speak from the floor of the House. It did not strike him that that question was not so much an exhibition of interest on his part as of ignorance. He asked it quite innocently, just as if it were something he could not possibly be expected to know. So I told him, gently, that the public - school children in America knew whether cabinet ministers in England spoke in the House, and that with us we considered knowing just such things part of the education of a gentleman, like knowing how to mount a lady on horseback, and that not to know them was as something to hide, like a soiled pair of cuffs, and of which it was proper to be ashamed. It was not that we looked up to these other nations and studied them in consequence, as the "saleslady" reads the society column which treats of the Four Hundred, but because with us we were expected to know of Freycinet and Caprivi and

Rudini and Gladstone, just as we were of Cleveland or Reed.

As Goethe says, "One only finds in Rome what one takes there." The Englishman takes nothing to America but himself. The American takes to England and the rest of Europe the accumulated learning of his lifetime, a quick interest, which is *not* curiosity, and a foreknowledge of the traditions and present daily life of what he sees. And so when he enters the House of Parliament he enters it with the full knowledge of all that it means and has meant for centuries. He sees the trial of Warren Hastings and the entrance of Cromwell; and the white marble statues along the corridor from the old Hall to the new House are alive to him, and pregnant with intelligence. He does *not* exclaim, "These are the halls of my ancestors," "Blood is thicker than water," and "I am only, after all, returning to mine inheritance."

That is the sort of stuff American consuls talk at London dinners. That is the way the Englishman bores one by trying to explain the interest one takes in his history.

"Ah, yes!" he says, "you feel that, after all, we are the same people."

Some Americans may feel that way, and thrill over it. I know one American who does not. It is not that we were once one people, but that the Houses of Parliament are something of

which we have read and heard, and are not
England's alone, but the world's. We would
thrill in the same way over the Pyramids or the
field of Marathon or the Champs-Elysées.

I once heard a dear old lady from the country
say to her equally dear old husband in a New
York horse-car, " Henry, do you appreciate the
fact that we are on Broadway?" Broadway to
her was a great name and place that she had
thought would be always a name, and she found
herself part of it, and it thrilled her simple old
heart. It was *not* because her great-grandfather
had once kept a shop on Broadway. And so
when we go into the gallery and look down on
all the men of whom we have heard so long we
feel things, and it is *not* because our great-grandfather once sat in those halls and made the laws
for their sovereign, but because we feel we are
watching men make history. But an Englishman cannot understand *that*.

It is impossible not to take advantage of a comparison already familiar and liken the interior of
the Houses of Parliament to a well-ordered club.
That is the simplest and most direct way of de-
scribing it. The decoration is no more serious
nor no more handsome than is that of some of
the older clubs on Pall Mall, and the attitude of
the ushers, or whatever those dignitaries are
called who look like bishops and wear gold chains,
who *think* they can get you the order of the day,

CHANGING GUARD AT ST. JAMES'S PALACE

and who are yet human enough to take even a shilling for doing so, is strongly suggestive of the club servant. The smoking-room is like any other smoking-room, with its leather cushions and electric buttons and red-waistcoated waiters, and the grill-room just as hot, over-lighted, and noisy as most club grill-rooms : and the tea on the terrace while the heavy barges with their brown sails and the penny excursion boats go by, and with Lambeth Palace across the way, is much more suggestive of the Lyric Club's terrace farther up the Thames than the breathing-ground of a great legislative body. I am sure the tea on that terrace has had much more influence on the politics of Great Britain than all the much stronger drinks served in the smoking-room below-stairs. And if it were wise to put a screen in front of the women in the House itself, it would seem even better wisdom to screen them off the terrace as well. They could not do very much harm from the gallery, even were the lattice taken away, but out there on the terrace, in the late English twilight, and with the moon perhaps hanging over St. Paul's, and all the various lights of the Surrey side and of the passing craft showing on the black surface of the river, they are very dangerous indeed. How many men, one might question, have decided that Conservatives were, after all, very nice people, and their wives and daughters at least most innocent, and that

Liberal - Unionist sounds better than Liberal,
which people *will* translate Radical, and that it
is rather pleasant to be taken up by such smart
people and to pour out tea for them.

The first impression one gets of the chamber
of the House of Commons is that it is so very
small. It does not surprise you to find the
House of Peers a hall of somewhat limited pro-
portions. That seems to be in keeping with the
exclusiveness of its members.

But the House of Commons sounds so momentous, and such great things have been carried out there, that one rather looks for something grand and imposing and impressive. And
when you take your place in the gallery, and
lean over the railing to look down upon the high
hats of the members, you feel that you are rather
in a private chapel than in a legislative hall, and
that by reaching out your hand you could almost touch the Speaker in his high chair, which
always wickedly suggested a Punch-and-Judy
show to me, and the top of which, I was grieved
to note, was not dusted.

I found it very hard at first to grasp the fact
that the gentlemen sitting on the benches or
walking in and out, and making little bows to
the Speaker whenever they did so, whether he
was looking at them or not, were the real men
themselves of whom we have read, and with
whom *Punch's* " Essence of Parliament " and the

illustrated papers have made us familiar. It was interesting to think you were hearing before any one else the speeches or the arguments that were to be read the next morning in America and India. Going to the House day after day was like a procession of " first nights " given with a star cast. I caught myself commenting with some surprise on how like the men were to their pictures, and that there really was a latticed grating, and that the shadowy, moving figures behind it, like the ghostly jury in " The Bells," were real women and young girls, guarded from view like slaves in a harem ; and that there were a mace and a gangway and a master-of-arms with a sword, just as Harry Furniss draws him, and a reporters' gallery, where Warrington and Charles Dickens once sat ; and that Mr. Balfour did wear gaiters, and Mr. Gladstone high-peaked collars ; and that the Irish members were as obnoxious as I had been led to believe they would be ; and that the Lord Chancellor in the Upper House looked just as he did in " Iolanthe."

It was like seeing one of Shakespeare's plays on the stage for the first time after one had studied it only from the book. What impressed me most about the House was the air of good-breeding which prevailed there, and the strictness of the etiquette—the fact that the members might not read a newspaper within its limits, and the courtesy with which they bowed and gave to each other the full title. It seemed so cosey and comfortable — legislation made easy, as it were — the colors were so harmonious and the coats of arms so numerous, and the ubiquitous policemen in the lobbies and halls outside so obsequious, that a member's life, one thought, must be a happy one. And they have such amusing privileges outside the House. Their hansoms may, for instance, go through any block at Waterloo Bridge, no matter how heavy the traffic may be, and if they are cabinet ministers they can go through a block anywhere. If I were a cabinet minister I would take a hansom by the hour, and spend my time riding around to find blocks that I might be let through, and so make other people envious. And inside the House they are allowed to ask their friends to dinner, and to wear their hats all the time and everywhere, even, or especially — for some of the Liberals are silly enough to make a point of it—when the Prince of Wales takes his seat in the gallery.

The most interesting moments in the House to one who is not so fortunate as to be present at any great debate is question-time, when members of both parties ask questions of the government. These questions, in order that they may be answered by the proper persons, require the actual presence of the greater number of the cabinet or of their under-secretaries, so that one hears and sees the most interesting men of the

party in power under fire, or at least on the de-
fensive. It used to be that a member could ask
a question of the government without giving any
warning as to what the question was to be; but
this privilege became so grossly abused by those
who asked only embarrassing questions meant to
embarrass that the questions were ordered to be
printed and sent in advance to the heads of the
different departments who were expected to answer them. This gave them some time to prepare their reply, and to avoid telling too much or
too little.

In the order of the day, which is furnished
the members at each sitting, these questions
now appear numbered and titled, with the name
of the man who is to ask them. When his
turn comes, he rises and takes off his hat, and
asks the Right Honorable the Secretary of State
for the Home Department, for instance, to answer question twenty-nine. Then the gentleman or his under-secretary makes a more or less
satisfactory answer in a very few words. The
value of these questions to the visitor is that
they show how far-reaching and multitudinous
are the interests of the House of Commons.
There no topic is so trivial that, if it concerns a
British subject, it is not important enough to
command the attention of the House, and you
get a glimpse of a paternal government which
one moment causes a smile, and the next fills you

with wonder at the greatness of the system that can reach out from Westminster and hold an army at check at the Khyber Pass, or protect the whaling-master in Bering Sea, or punish a policeman on the Strand. Nothing is too little to escape its notice, and nothing too momentous to baffle its inquiry. The latter fact is not remarkable; that seems the natural burden of the House of Commons. But it must always strike the American as amusing that so great a legislative body should take up its own time in the consideration of matters which a police justice could adjust as satisfactorily.

The Irish members last summer were, as a rule, the most aggressive in their inquiries and their questions the most trivial. I had, as I suppose every American has, a sentimental interest in home-rule until I had seen something of the men who stood for it. Those who are its champions this year, now that the other party is in power, and since home-rule has become a government measure, are no doubt a very different class, but the Irish members of 1892 seemed to me capable of doing their cause as much harm as any member of the opposition could have possibly hoped to accomplish. They were the representatives in the House of a great question, a great measure, the most important that has obtained the attention of the House for many years, and instead of saving their strength for this and bearing them-

COACHES AT WHITEHALL

selves in such a manner as to gain the respect and admiration even of their opponents, as they might have done had they been big men capable of carrying out a big reform, or at least a great change, they disgusted even their friends, and were nothing to their opponents but annoying mischief-makers. They seemed to indicate by their manner—and very bad manners they were —that they intended to misbehave, no matter how polite the others might be—in spite of that fact, indeed. They reminded me of spoiled chil-

dren who were proud of the fact that they were
the worst boys in the school, and would *not* be
good even were it to attain their own ends. And
so they were a trial to those who were sincere,
who were in earnest, and who had far less at
stake, and a burden to their friends and a delight
to their enemies. Englishmen might as fairly
ask us to put the national government into the
hands of the Tammany sachems as for us to expect them to give the control of Ireland to the
men I saw last year at Westminster. This is not
a popular way of looking at it in America. But
no cause is better than the men who represent
it; at least they can hardly expect others to
judge it by any higher basis than their own showing.

The only copy of the orders of the day which
I have kept with me is the one for the 13th of
June, 1892. I did not keep it with any intent,
but it shows excellently well the character and
conduct of the Irish members, and illustrates also
what I have said about the variety of interests
with which the House concerns itself. On that
day it appears that there were thirty questions
on the programme. Twenty of these were asked
by the Irish members alone; that is, two-thirds
of question-time was taken up by a half-dozen
men out of the six hundred and seventy members. If these questions were legitimate and
sincere one could only applaud the interest of

the Irish member on behalf of his constituents, but questions like these seem hardly worth while:

12. Mr. Sexton,—To ask the Postmaster - General whether he is aware that the surveyor for the northern district of Ireland refused to forward a petition from the postal staff of the Belfast office because the petition was a printed one:

Whether there is any rule which directs that petitions should be in manuscript:

And whether any English surveyor has refused to forward a similar petition on the same ground.

36. Dr. Tanner,—To ask the chief secretary to the Lord Lieutenant of Ireland whether any steps have been taken to obtain a site for a cottage under the laborers (Ireland) acts in the parish of Doneraile, County Cork, near Oldcourt graveyard, and if he is aware that a site was chosen by the dispensary committee, approved by the engineer to the union, but obstructed by a local tenant farmer:

And whether, in view of the fact that the provision of this cottage has been repeatedly asked for by the people of the locality, the local government board will take steps to settle the matter.

5. Mr. William O'Brien,—To ask the Secretary of State for War whether he is aware that Martin O'Donnell, at the date of his enlistment in the Connaught Rangers at Galway, was under the prescribed age for recruits:

And whether, having regard to the fact that this young lad of seventeen years of age is the only support of a widowed mother, who has eight other young children, he will order O'Donnell's discharge.

19. Mr. Patrick O'Brien,—To ask the chief secretary to the Lord Lieutenant of Ireland whether he is aware that the cow of a laborer named Michael Traynor, of Creerylake, near Carrickmacross, County Monaghan, was seized on the 4th instant by a bailiff named Henry Stubs when trespassing on an evicted farm on the Shirely estate and impounded, and that Stubs detained the animal for three days, and charged the owner £3 before releasing it:

And what was the charge of £3 for, and was it a legal charge.

Imagine the interests of an empire standing idle while its representative body considers the case of a cow, of a single recruit, and of the site of a thatched cottage. Some of the other questions of that day show the extent of these interests, and that the House of Commons is as omnipotent as an Eastern Sultan who decides upon going to war or upon the case of a shoemaker who will not pay his debts.

21. Major-General Goldsworthy,—To ask the Under-Secretary of State for India whether India is to be represented at the Chicago Exhibition ; and if so, whether the government of India proposes to give a grant in aid.

11. Mr. Norris,—To ask the First Lord of the Admiralty what inducements, if any, are held out to

the junior officers of the navy to acquire foreign languages, and if periodical examinations are held :

And if he is aware that French officers who visited England last year expressed surprise at the deficiency in this respect of the English naval officers.

23. Mr. Henniker Heaton,—To ask the Postmaster-General the exact date and hour of the arrival of the Orient steamship *Orotava* at Naples last week, at what hour the mails left Naples for London, and the cause of the delay in their arrival here.

20. Mr. Sexton,—To ask the Secretary of State for the Home Department if it has been brought to his knowledge that on the 5th of February last Catherine O'Toole, a weaver, had one of her eyes destroyed by a blow from the shuttle of a loom beside where she was working in the weaving factory of the Belfast Flax Spinning and Weaving Company (Limited), Waterford Street, Belfast; that another weaver, named Lizzie Boyd, had one of her eyes destroyed in the same way in the weaving factory of the York Street Spinning Company (Limited), Belfast, on the 3d of May :

Were those injuries caused by the neglect of the employers or their superintendents to have suitable screens erected at each end of the loom so as to prevent the shuttle flying out in case of accident:

And whether the government, having regard to the frequency of such accidents, will cause to be appointed as inspector of factories in Belfast a tenter or other person recommended by the Belfast Trades Council, and having practical knowledge and experience of the working of such looms.

16. Major-General Goldsworthy,—To ask the Un-

der-Secretary of State for Foreign Affairs whether he
is aware that in December last, before the provisional
regulations were issued, a petition was signed by ship
owners representing over 5,000,000 tons of shipping,
protesting against the passage of petroleum - tank
steamers through the Suez Canal.

10. Sir Guyer Hunter,—To ask the Under-Secretary
of State for India whether the rank of medical officers
mentioned in Article 267A of the recent royal warrant,
as carrying " precedence and other advantages indi-
cated by the military portion of the title," has been
infringed by a recent ruling of the commander-in-chief
of the Bombay army, relative to the position at mess
of medical officers organically belonging to native
regiments in India, in which it is declared that the
senior combatant officer present takes military precedence on all occasions ; and if such ruling be valid,
what is the precise nature and scope of the " precedence " set forth in the article quoted of the royal
warrant.

39. Mr. Causton,—To ask the President of the
Board of Trade whether he can inform the House how
many boats and the number of people they would ac-
commodate were carried by the steamer *Albert Edward*
at the time of the recent collision on the passage from
Boulogne to Folkestone :

And how many passengers were on board the
steamer at the time of the collision.

These latter questions show the actual variety
of the interests of the House, and the paternal
nature of a government which inquires into the

doings and wants of its subjects from Chicago to
the Suez Canal, and from Bombay to Boulogne.

The next step is from the House to the Park
in time to see the parade of carriages, which is
possibly less interesting than the people who
gather to look at it. Fashion has moved slowly
but surely from west of Hyde Park Corner to
Stanhope Gate, and has left its original gathering-
ground to country cousins and foreigners, who sit
like people in a theatre, clutching the little penny
ticket which entitles them to a seat over a most
extensive area, and gazing open-eyed at the procession of fine horses and haughty ladies and
still haughtier coachmen. The smart people
haunted the lawn opposite Stanhope Gate last
year, and that they were left to themselves and
that no one not of their class came to stare at
them is one of the curious facts that an American cannot understand. If it were the rule and if
it were understood in New York that all of the
Few Hundred intended to occupy a certain portion of the Park at a certain hour of each afternoon, it would not be very long before all the
nurse-maids would circle it with their perambula-
tors, and people not of the Few Hundred would
go there too, some of them because they wished
to stare at the people whose names they had read
in the "society" column, and some because they
wished to show that the Park belonged equally
to them, whatever their social standing might be.

But this is not the case in London. The lawn opposite Stanhope Gate is as free as the air to any one who pays his penny for a green chair, but no one not of a certain class goes there. They sit below, recognizing an invisible barrier; they would not be comfortable opposite Stanhope Gate. This indefinable and unwritten right of the upper class to keep to itself is very interesting. Under that tree the Duchess of —— always sat; in this corner of the iron railing one was always sure to find the American heiress; and in the angle of the railing the Hon. Mrs. —— held her court and received her devotees. No one reserved these places, and yet every one recognized their right to them, as they recognize Mr. Gladstone's right to the corner seat of the first bench in the House. It is even more strongly illustrated at Brighton. There is a long parade there, stretching for miles along the shore; part of it is asphalt, and a little space is laid out in turf. There is no railing around the turf, no barrier of any sort, or any sign to mark it as being sacred soil, but no housemaid or landlady, or even the most quiet-looking of the women from "the Wood," would think of walking there. It is reserved for the smart people by some unwritten law, and the rest of the world not of their world recognizes this and keeps off the grass and walks on the asphalt.

The spot opposite Stanhope Gate looked more

like a private lawn-party than a public park.
We have nothing like that at home. The Clare-
mont teas had to be fenced in with cards of admittance, and they were somewhat spoiled by
the blasting of rock in the near neighborhood,
and the sight of the Harlem goat and shanty
within a few hundred yards. Exclusiveness is
not allowed to enjoy a healthy growth undis-
turbed in our republican garden.

The sights of London at night do not begin
until very late on account of the delightfully late
twilights, and end very abruptly at midnight on
account of the police. But when the hansoms
begin to flash past by the thousands, and the
theatres open up their doors like open fireplaces
in the night, and the policemen's lanterns throw
long lines of light, the city is nearly at its best.
It seems to hold such a potential possibility of
adventure and romance ; it becomes mysterious
and momentous, and yet widely awake and brilliant. You feel that every one has laid aside the
burden of the day, and is intent on pleasure or
on entertainment. The swift rush of the hansoms, even when they have no fare inside, always
struck me as being the most significant sign of
the hour, as though even the horses knew that
it would all go out in a little while and they
must make the best of their time.

London has wisely divided her sources of public amusements in the evening between the music-

halls and the theatres. To the theatre go the properly clothed men and women from late dinners, conscious and considerate of those who may sit behind them, and of the fitness of things in fine linen and bare shoulders. To the halls go the less critical and less particular. I, personally, preferred the halls, for the reason that the audience is a part of the entertainment, and that one can learn the feelings of the Englishman on any public question much more at first hand there than by reading what he is told to think in the leading editorial columns of the papers. It is significant, for instance, when a comic singer is not allowed to continue for three minutes because he has referred to Mr. Gladstone as the Grand Old Woman, and when a plea in verse for Mrs. Maybrick draws forth cheers, and a figure made up to look like Lord Salisbury elicits shouts of derisive laughter. It was in the music-hall that a comic singer gave a new name to the Conservative party by singing, "We don't want to fight, but by jingo," etc., and it is in the halls that the young Briton is taught to sing, "God bless the Prince and Princess of Wales," and to hoot at the German Prince Henry of Battenberg.

I have heard a comic singer stop the orchestra and say to the audience: "I don't think you could have undersood that last verse. The line was, 'And drive these German boors away.' Some of you applauded; you mustn't do that.

You must hiss that line. Now we will try that over again ; and don't forget to hiss." At which he would repeat the verse, and the audience would hoot and hiss at the appropriate sentiment. Some paper—*Punch*, I think it was—described Lord Randolph Churchill as going from shop-window to shop-window counting the number of his photographs exposed for sale, in order to compare them with those offered of Letty Lind and Mr. Gladstone, and so gauge his popularity. If an English politician really wishes to know what the people think of him, he should give up subscribing to a newspaper - clipping agency and attend the music-halls. He would get a very good idea of his popularity there.

The sentiment of the music - hall song differs according to location. A Conservative song will go well around Leicester Square in the West End, but will be hissed on the Surrey side or in Islington. So some of the performers endeavor to please both parties by giving each a verse, and then adding a third of a strongly national and patriotic nature, which draws both factions together and leaves the actor without suspicion of partiality for any particular party. As, for instance, there is one in which the singer tells of his asking Lord Salisbury how Mr. Gladstone came to lose his place ; this was sung, of course, before the last general election, and to which the Premier, being no doubt in an affable mood

and without suspecting that the music-hall man
was going to repeat what had been told him, in-
forms him that it was

> " All through his greed of office.
>   All through his love of power.
>   What cares he for old England's rights?
>   The Liberal party he disunites.
>   For what? For the votes of the Parnellites.
>   *That's* how he lost his place."

This is received with cheers by the Conservatives and hoots by the Liberals, which latter the
comic singer hastens to appease by going direct
to Mr. Gladstone himself and asking him for his
side of it.   He addresses him in this way:

> "'How did you lose your place, great sire?
>   How did you lose your place?'
>   I asked of England's Grand Old Man
>   With the kind and careworn face.
>   His gentle eyes looked into mine,
>   And, pausing for a moment's time,
>   He answered, with a smile sublime:
> 'Why did I lose my place?
>   All for the sake of Ireland,
>   All for the Emerald Isle.
>   I've seen the world and my friends grow cool;
>   In my old, old age they call me a fool;
>   But I'll live to see Ireland gain home-rule,
>   And they'll give me back my place.'"

This song, sung to a very stirring melody, has often brought the performance on the stage to a close for fully three minutes, while the audience expressed themselves with energy. And yet we call the Englishman stolid and unemotional. Imagine an American audience going quite crazy because a comic song spoke disrespectfully of one or the other of the Presidential candidates! But it has a healthy, patriotic quality about it which is most pleasing, as is shown on the last verse of this same song. In this the singer, who is of an inquiring mind apparently, asks an "aged veteran" how he came to lose his arm, and the veteran replies:

  "'Fighting at Balaclava,
    Fighting for England's fame.
    I was in front when the charge was made
    Where the cannon roared
    And the sabres played,
    Riding to death with the Light Brigade.
    That's how I lost my arm.'"

With a fine brass band playing the accompaniment, and a large drum to represent the cannon, and a man to sing the words with a barytone voice, this last verse is calculated to make even the casual foreigner stand up and shout. On the whole, I consider the music-hall a much misunderstood and undervalued entertainment. It fosters other things besides patriotism, though;

its devotees are neither innocent nor ignorant
of the world's ways. But "the halls," as one of
the show things of London, have their proper
place.

They are not always the noisy, smoke-filled
places one pictures them. They are like any other
theatre, with gorgeous plush seats and great di-
vans and velvet curtains and proudly uniformed
attendants, and some of their stars are artists who
draw as much as one hundred pounds a week, and
drive around the streets from hall to hall in smart
broughams, with "Vesta Tilly, the Vital Spark,"
or the "Sisters Bilton," painted on the lamps in
red letters. They are often extremely vulgar,
and as frequently as dull; but there is always
something to redeem the rest — an artist like
Albert Chevalier, or a countess who sings queer
songs, or the friend of a noble duke who stops
singing to take the house into her confidence
and tell them of her private difficulties, and who is
hailed, consolingly, as "Good old Bessie," because,
I suppose, she is not old, and certainly not good;
or a man like Rowley or Connors, who sings
songs in which the entire house joins; and I can
assure those who have not heard six or seven
hundred men singing the chorus of a comic song
that it has a most interesting effect.

The show part of London ends, in the West
End at least, at midnight. It can be continued
behind club doors after that, but, as far as the

streets are concerned, London is either an impossible place in which to walk or a wilderness. To a clubless visitor it is the most inhospitable city in the world. Not even a restaurant is open to him, and, for all he can see outside of the closed doors, the curtain is down and the show is over. This is the strangest feature almost of this great city, its prompt good-night at twelve o'clock.

V

THE WEST AND EAST ENDS OF LONDON

T has seemed so difficult to write of the social side of the London season that I have put off saying anything of it until now. It is necessary to touch upon it here, or to leave it out of consideration altogether. To do the latter would be like writing of the Horse Show and omitting everything but the horses, and to do the former puts the writer in the unpleasant light of criticising those who have been civil to him. It may be possible, and I hope it may prove so, to avoid speaking of the social side of the London season in anything but generalities.

Of course the most obvious differences between the season in London and the season in New York are due to the difference in the season of the year. We cannot give garden-parties in

December or February, nor, were the American fashionables given to that form of amusement, can they go to race meetings in January. Hence the out-of-door life of a London season — the lawn-parties in town, the water-parties on the Thames, the church parade, and the gatherings in the Row in the morning and on the lawn opposite Stanhope Gate before dinner, the week at Ascot, and the closing of the season at Goodwood—is of a kind with which there is nothing similar to compare in New York. The elements of fashionable life which are most alike in both cities are the dinners and dances and the opera. Dinners, I imagine, are pretty much the same all the world over, and the dances in London, at the first glance, are like as smart dances in New York, as far as the young people and the music and the palms and the supper and such things go. There is, however, a very marked difference in the solemnity of the young Englishmen and in the shyness and sedateness of the young girls. There are certain interests to offset this, which are lacking with us, one of which is the number of married women you see whose faces are already familiar to you on both sides of the Atlantic through their photographs in shop windows, and who keep you wondering where you have come across them and their tiaras before, and another is the greater number of servants, whose livery and powdered hair add color to the halls, and who, when they pass on the word that "Lady Somebody's carriage blocks the way," are much more picturesque than Johnson in his ulster and high hat calling out " 3 West Madison Square." There is a more brilliant showing of precious stones in London, and the older men in the sashes and stars of the different orders of the empire add something of color and distinction which we do not have at home. Otherwise the scene is much the same.

It is only when you leave the ballroom and go out on the lawn or into the surrounding rooms that you come across an anomaly which is most disturbing. The American girl who seeks corners and tops of stairways, or who, when the weather permits, wanders away from the lighted rooms and the care of her chaperon into the garden around the house, if the house has a garden, is sure to suffer the penalty of being talked about. Young married women may do that sort of thing with us, but a young girl must remain in evidence, she must be where her partners can reach her, and where whoever is looking after her can whisper to her to hold herself straight, or that she is dancing her hair down. If she wants to talk to a man alone, as she sometimes does, and her mother approves of the man, she can see him at her own home over a cup of tea any afternoon after five. But she cannot do this if she is an English girl in London. So when the English

"YOU ARE CONSTANTLY INTRUDING"

girl goes to a dance at a private house she takes
advantage of the long waits between each dance,
which are made very long on purpose, and rushes
to all parts of the house, or out into the garden,
where she sits behind statues and bushes. So,
when you wander out for a peaceful smoke, you
are constantly intruding upon a gleaming shirt-
front and the glimmer of a white skirt hidden
away in the surrounding canopy of green. It is
most embarrassing. I had been brought up to
believe that English girls were the most overrid-
den and over-chaperoned young women in the
world, and I still think they are, except in this
one particular license allowed them at dances.
It struck me as most contradictory and somewhat absurd. Why, if a young girl may not see
a young man alone at her own house, should she
be allowed to wander all over some other person's house with him? It seems to me that it is
in much better taste to do as we do and let the
girl see the man under her own roof.

The most novel feature of the dance in London, which does not obtain with us, is the sudden changing of night into day, at the early hour
of two in the morning. Daylight obtrudes so
late in New York that it is generally the signal
for going home; but it comes so early in the
game in London that one often sees the cotillon
begun in a clear sunlight, which does not mar,
but rather heightens, the beauty of the soft Eng-

lish complexions and the fair arms and shoulders of the young girls, even while it turns the noblest son and heir of the oldest house into something distressingly like a waiter.

This is one of the prettiest sights in London. A roomful of young girls, the older women having discreetly fled before the dawn, romping through a figure in the smartest of *décolleté* gowns, and in the most brilliant sunlight, with the birds chirping violently outside, and the fairy-lamps in the gardens smoking gloomily, and the Blue Hungarian Band yawning over their fiddles. It is all very well for the women, but, as one of the men said, "I always go home early now; one hates to have people one knows take one for a butler and ask after their carriage."

There is a decorum about an English dance which, I should think, will always tend to keep the hostess in doubt as to whether or not her guests have enjoyed themselves as keenly as they assure her they have done when they murmur their adieus. And I do not mean by this that there is any indecorum at a dance in America, but there is less consciousness of self, and more evident enjoyment of those things which are meant to be enjoyed, and no such terribly trying exhibitions of shyness.

Shyness, it struck me, is the most remarkable of all English characteristics. It is not a pretty trait. It is a thing which is happily almost un-

known to us.   The Englishman will agree to
this with a smile because he thinks that we are
too bold, and because he believes that shyness
is a form of modesty.   It is nothing of the sort.
It is simply a sign of self-consciousness, and,
in consequence, of bad breeding; it is the very
acme of self-consciousness, and carries with it its
own punishment.   People with us are either reserved or over-confident, or simple and sincere,
or bold and self-assertive; but they are not shy.
And what is most aggravating is that the English make shyness something of a virtue, and
think that it covers a multitude of sins.   If a
man is rude or a woman brusque, his or her
friends will say, "You mustn't mind him, he's so
shy," or, "She doesn't mean anything; that's
just her manner; she's so shy."   The English
are constantly laughing mockingly at their
French neighbor on account of his manner, and
yet his exaggerated politeness is much less trying to one's nerves than the average Englishman's lack of the small-change of conversation
and his ever-present self-consciousness, which
render him a torment to himself and a trial to
the people he meets.

There are different kinds of shyness, and dif
ferent causes for it.   To be quite fair, it is only
right to say that in many cases the Englishman's
shyness is due to his desire not to appear egotis-
tical, nor to talk of himself, or of what he does,

13

or happens to have done.   His horror of the appearance of boasting is so great that he often errs in the other direction, and is silent or abrupt in order that he may not be drawn into speaking of himself, or of appearing to give importance to his own actions.   Modesty is, I think, the most charming of all English characteristics, only it is in some instances overdone.   In our country a man likes you to refer to the influence he wields: he likes you to say, "A man in your position," or, "Any one with your influence," or, "Placed as you are, you could if you would."   It is the breath of his nostrils to many a man.

But an Englishman detests any reference to the fact that he is an important personage as if it were something over which he ought to be pleased; he wears his honors awkwardly; more frequently he leaves them at home.   He does not wear his war medals with civilian dress.   He is quite honest in his disregard of title if he has one, though, being mortal, he thinks as much of it if he lacks it as the chance American does. But he does not say, "Come down to *my* house and ride *my* horses and look at *my* pictures."   If he takes you over his place, he is apt to speak of his ancestor's tomb as a "jolly old piece of work," just as though it were a sundial or a chimney-piece, and he is much more likely to show you the family skeleton than the family plate and pictures.

I was in a boy's room at Oxford last summer, and saw a picture of one of the peers of England there, a man who has held the highest offices in the diplomatic service. "Why do you have such a large picture of Lord —— here?" I asked. "Do you admire him as much as that?"

"He's my father," he said. "Of course," he went on, anxiously, "he doesn't dress in all those things unless he has to. Here is a better portrait of him."

And he showed me one of his father in knickerbockers. It struck me as a very happy instance of English reserve about those things of which the average American youth would have been apt to speak. I had known him a couple of weeks, but on account of his bearing the family name I did not connect him with his father. The "things" to which he referred were the grand crosses of the orders of the Bath, and of the Star of India, and of the Indian Empire. An American boy would have pointed out their significance to you; but the English boy proffered the picture of his father in a tweed suit instead.

I have heard Americans in London tell very long stories of our civil war, and of their very large share in bringing it to a conclusion, and as no one had asked them to talk about it, or knew anything about it, it used to hurt my feelings, especially as I remembered that I had tried to drag anecdotes of the Soudan and India out of the several English officers present, and without success. So, on the whole, one must remember this form of shyness too. But the shyness which comes from stupid fear is unpardonable.

As an American youth said last summer, " It is rather disappointing to come over here prepared to bow down and worship, and to find you have to put a duchess at her ease." I asked an Englishman once whether or not people shook hands when they were introduced in England. I told him we did not do so at home, but that English people seemed to have no fixed rule about it, and I wanted to know what was expected. " Well, you know," he said, with the most charming naïveté, " it isn't a matter of rule exactly ; one is generally so embarrassed when being introduced that one really doesn't know whether one is shaking hands or not." And he quite expected me to agree with him.

If the English themselves were the only ones to suffer from their own lack of ease, and of the little graces which oil the social wheels, it would not so much matter ; one would only regret that they were not having a more agreeable time. But they make others suffer, especially the stranger within their gates. Mr. Robert Louis Stevenson, in his essay on " The Foreigner at Home," tells of the trials of the Scotchman when he first visits England. He says: " A Scotchman is vain, interested in himself and

"PEOPLE ONE KNOWS TAKE ONE FOR A BUTLER"

others, eager for sympathy, setting forth his thoughts and experience in the best light. The egotism of the Englishman is self-contained. He does not seek to proselytize. He takes no interest in Scotland or the Scotch, and, what is the unkindest cut of all, he does not care to justify his indifference."

If the Scotchman, who certainly seems reserved enough in our eyes, is chilled by the Englishman's manner, it is evident how much more the American must suffer before he learns that there is something better to come, and that the Englishman's manner is his own misfortune and not his intentional fault. The Englishman says to this, when you know him well enough to complain, that we are too "sensitive," and that we are too quick to take offence. It never occurs to him that it may be that he is too brusque. If you say, on mounting a coach, "I am afraid I am one too many, I fear I am crowding you all," you can count upon their all answering, with perfect cheerfulness, " Yes, you are, but we didn't know you were coming, and there is no help for it." It never occurs to them that that is not perhaps the best way of putting it. After a bit you find out that they do not mean to be rude, or you learn to be rude yourself, and then you get on famously.

I have had Americans come into my rooms in London with tears of indignation in their eyes, and tell of the way in which they had been, as they supposed, snubbed and insulted and neglected.

"Why," they would ask, "did they invite me to their house if they meant to treat me like that? I didn't ask them to invite me. I didn't force myself on them. I only wanted a word now and then, just to make me feel I was a human being. If they had only asked me, 'When are you going away?' it would have been something; but to leave me standing around in corners, and to go through whole dinners without as much as a word, without introducing me to any one or recognizing my existence— Why did they ask me if they only meant to insult me when they got me there? Is that English hospitality?"

And the next day I would meet the people with whom he had been staying, and they would say, "We have had such a nice compatriot of yours with us, such a well-informed young man; I hope he will stop with us for the shooting."

As far as they knew they had done all that civility required, all that they would have done for their neighbors, or would have expected from their own people. But they did not know that we are not used to being walked over rough-shod, that we affect interest even if we do not feel it, and that we tell social fibs if it is going to make some one else feel more comfortable. It is as if the American had boxed with gloves all his life, and then met a man who struck with his bare fists; and it naturally hurts. And the most pathetic part of the whole thing is that they do not know how much better than their own the breeding of the American really is. It is like the line in the *International Episode*, where the American woman points out to her friend that their English visitors not only dress badly, but so badly that they will not appreciate how well dressed the Americans are. I have seen a whole roomful of Englishmen sit still when a woman came into her own drawing-room, and then look compassionately at the Americans present because they stood up. They probably thought that we were following out the rules of some book on etiquette, and could not know that we were simply more comfortable standing when a woman was standing than we would have been sitting down.

And it will not do to say in reply to this that these Englishmen of whom I speak were not of the better sort, and that I should not judge by the middle class. I am not writing of the middle classes. "It was the best butter," as the March hare says.

I have had Americans tell me, and most interesting Americans they were, of dinners in London where they had sat, after the women left the room, in absolute isolation, when the men near them turned their backs on them, and talked of

things interesting only to themselves, and left the
stranger to the mercies of the butler. Imagine
anything like that with us! Imagine our neg-
lecting a guest to that extent—and an Englishman too! We might not like him, and probably
would find him a trifle obtuse, but we would not
let him see it, and we would at least throw him
a word now and again, and ask him if he meant
to shoot big game, or merely to write a book
about us. It might be that we never intended to read his book, or cared whether he shot
moose or himself, but as long as he was our guest
we would try to make him feel that we did not
consider our responsibility was at an end when
we gave him bread-and-butter. But the average
Englishman and English woman does not feel
this responsibility.

I remember a dinner given in New York last
winter to a prominent Englishman who was visiting this country, when there happened to be a
number of very clever men at the table who were
good after-dinner talkers, and not after-dinner
story-tellers, which is a vastly different thing.
The Englishman's contribution to the evening's
entertainment was a succession of stories which
he had heard on this side, and which he told
very badly. The Americans were quite able to
judge of this, as they had told the stories themselves many different times. But they all listened with the most serious or amused interest,

and greeted each story with the proper amount
of laughter, and by saying, " How very good,"
and " Quite delightful!" Then they all reached
under the table and kicked the shins of the unhappy host who had subjected them to this trial.

In England it would not have been the host
nor his English friends who would have suffered.

I went with a man who had never been in
London before to a garden-party last summer,
and warned him on the way that he would not
be introduced to any one, and that after he had
met his hostess he would probably be left rooted
to a block of stone on the terrace, and would
be as little considered as a marble statue. He
smiled scornfully at this, but half an hour after
our arrival I passed him for the third time as he
stood gazing dreamily out across the park just
where I had left him. And as I passed he
dropped the point of his stick to the ground,
and drew it carefully around the lines of the slab
of marble upon which he was standing, and then
continued to smile peacefully out across the
lawn. I do not think they treat us in this way
because we are Americans, but because we are
strangers, and London is a very busy place, and
a very big place, and those who go about there
have their time more than taken up already, and
have but little to spare for the chance visitor.
They treat their own people in the same way.
The governor's lady of some little island or mili-

tary station in the colonies, who has virtually boarded and lodged and danced and wined the distinguished English family who visited the station in their yacht last winter, thinks, poor thing, when she reaches London that she will receive favors in return, and sends her card expectingly, as she has been urged not to forget to do, and she is invited to luncheon. And after luncheon her hostess says: "Good-bye. We are going to Lady Somebody's musical. Shall we see you there? No? Then we shall meet again, I hope." But unless they meet at a street crossing, it is unlikely.

It is the same with those young English subalterns who come back from India and Egypt tanned and handsome and keen for the pleasures of the town, and who have been singing for years, "When will we see London again?" and find their three months' furlough slipping by with nothing to show for it but clubs and theatres, and who go back abusing the country and the town that have failed to mark their return or to take note of their presence. I know one woman in London who expends her energies in asking cards for things for young lieutenants back on leave, who appoints herself their hostess, whose pleasure is in giving these young men pleasure, and who makes them think the place they call home has not forgotten them. When they have gone back to the barracks or the jungle, they have more to

'NOTHING TO SHOW FOR IT BUT CLUBS AND THEATRES'

thank her for than they know, and many pleasant things to remember. I rather like her missionary work better than that of Dr. Bernando.

There are a great many Americans who will tell you that we, as Americans, are very popular in London; that the English think us clever and amusing on account of our "quaint American humor," and our too-curious enthusiasm over their traditions and their history and its monuments. It may be that I am entirely mistaken, but I do not think that we are popular at all. I think we are just the contrary. As for our American humor, they do not understand what is best of it, and they laugh, if they laugh at all, not with us, but at us. Those Americans who are willing to be a success through being considered buffoons, are perfectly welcome to become so, but it does not strike me as an edifying social triumph. The Americans who are very much liked in London, whether men or women, are not the Americans of whose doings we hear at home; they are not likely to furnish the papers with the material for cablegrams, and do not take the fact that they have been found agreeable by agreeable people as something of so surprising a nature that they should talk about it when they return to their own country.

As a matter of fact, I think the English care less for Americans than they do for any other foreigners. They think us pushing, given to overmuch bragging, and too self-assertive. They judge us a good deal by the Americans they meet at Homburg, who give large tips to the head waiter to secure the tables near that of a certain royal personage at luncheon-time ; or by those whom they chance to meet in a railway carriage, and who spend the time in telling them, uninvited, how vastly inferior are their travelling accommodations to those of the Chicago limited express, with its " barber shop, bath-room, type-writer, and vestibule-cars, sir, all in one." I used to get so weary of the virtues of this American institution that I vowed I would walk the ties when I returned home sooner than enter its rub-ber portals again. You can see what they think of our bragging by the anecdotes they tell you, which are supposed to be characteristic of Ameri-cans, and the point of which, when there is a point, invariably turns on some absurdly prodi-gious or boasting lie which one American tells another.

They also judge us a great deal, and, not un-naturally, by what we say of each other, and one cannot blame them for thinking that those of us whom they meet in town during the season must be a very bad lot.

It is almost as impossible to hear one Ameri-can speak well of another American in London as to hear the cock crow at dinner-time. " Oh, she's over here, is she?" they say, smiling myste-

riously. "No, I don't know her. She's not exactly—well, I really shouldn't say anything about
her; she is not a person I would be likely to
meet at home." I used to get so tired of hearing one American abuse another because he happened to know a duchess that the other one did
not know, because she was asked to a country-
house to which the other wanted to go, that I
made it a rule to swear that every man about
whom they asked me was considered in America
as one of the noblest of God's handiworks, and I
am afraid now that I may have vouched for some
very disreputable specimens. They were not
worse, however, than those Englishmen who
come to us each winter vouched for by equerries
of the Queen and several earls each, and who go
later to the Island in our cast-off shoes and with
some of our friends' money. If the English
judged us by the chance American and we judged
them by the average English adventurer, we
would go to war again for some reason or other
at once. And yet that is almost what we do.
We judge by the men who make themselves conspicuous, who force themselves on our notice,
whether they do it by bragging offensively in a
railway carriage, or by borrowing money, or fail-
ing to pay their club dues. We forget that the
gentleman, whether he comes from New York or
London or Athens, is not conspicuous, but passes
by unheard, like the angels we entertain una-

14

wares, and that where a gentleman is concerned there can be no international differences. There can only be one sort of a gentleman : there can be all varieties of cads. An Englishman used to argue last summer that he was quite fair in judging the Americans as a people by the average American, and not by those he is pleased to like and respect. He said they were not "representative" Americans, and that we could not argue that our best exponents of what Americans should and could be should represent us, which was of course quite absurd. When the English enter a yacht for an international race they enter their best yacht, not the third or fourth rate yachts. No women are more intelligent and womanly and sweet, and with a quicker sense of humor, than the best of the American women ; and no men that I have met anywhere more truly courteous and clever than the best American men ; and it is by these we should be judged, not by the American who scratches his name over cathedrals when the verger isn't looking, nor the young women who race through the halls of the Victoria Hotel.

All of this of which I have been speaking refers to the Englishman's manner, his outside, his crust, his bark, and bears in no way upon his spirit of hospitality which it disguises, but which is, nevertheless, much his best point, and in which he far outshines his American cousin. If you question this, consider what he gives, and how generously he gives it, in comparison with what we give to him. Of course hospitality is not to be judged or gauged by its expense, nor by how much one makes by it. The mere asking a man to sit down may breathe a truer hospitality than inviting him to consider all that is yours his, as the Spaniards do.

What do we for the visiting Englishman who comes properly introduced, and with a wife who happens to be his own? We ask him to dinner, and put him up at the clubs, and get invitations to whatever is going on, sometimes to give him pleasure, and sometimes to show him how socially important we may happen to be. In doing any of these things we run no great risk, we are not placed in a position from which we cannot at any moment withdraw. He does much more than this for the visiting American. For some time, it is true, he holds you at arm's-length, as I have just described; he looks you over and considers you, and is brusque or silent with you; and then, one fine day, when you have despaired of ever getting the small change of every-day politeness from him, he, figuratively speaking, stuffs your hands with bank-notes, and says, "That's all I have at present; spend it as you like, and call on me for more when it is gone." He takes you to his house and makes you feel it is your home. He gives you his servants, his house, his grounds,

his horses, his gun, and his keepers, and the society of his wife and daughters, and passes you
on eventually to his cousins and his sisters and
his brothers.   This is a show of confidence
which makes a dinner and a theatre party, or a
fortnight's privileges at a club, seem rather small.

It is true he does not meet you at the door
with his family grouped about him as though
they were going to be photographed, and with
the dogs barking a welcome; he lets you come
as you would come to your own house, as naturally and with as little ostentation.   But you
are given to understand when you are there that
as long as you turn up at dinner at the right
hour you are to do as you please.   You get up
when you like, and go to bed when you like;
you can fish for pike in the lake in front of the
house, or pick the flowers, or play tennis with
his sons and daughters, or read in his library, or
take the guide-book and wander over the house
and find out which is the Rubens, and trace the
family likeness on down to the present day by
means of Sir Joshua and Romney to Herkomer
and Watts, and Mendelssohn in a silver frame
on the centre table.   He has much more to
give than we have, and he gives it entirely and
without reserve; he only asks that you will enjoy
yourself after your own fashion, and allow him
to go on in his own house in his own way.
When a man has as much as this to give, you

SATURDAY NIGHT IN THE EAST END

cannot blame him if he does not cheapen it for
himself and for others by throwing it open to
whoever comes in his way.   The club with the
longest waiting list is generally the best club.

All of this is rather far away from the London season of which I began to write, but it is
the manners and characteristics of people which
make society, even fashionable society, and not
Gunter or Sherry.   You may forget whether it
was the regimental band of the First or Second
Lifeguards, but you do not forget that the hostess was gracious or rude.

The East End of London is entirely too awful,
and too intricate a neighborhood to be dismissed
in a chapter.   It is the back yard of the greatest
city in the world, into which all the unpleasant
and unsightly things are thrown and hidden
away from sight, to be dragged out occasionally
and shaken before the eyes of the West End as
a warning or a menace.   Sometimes, or all of the
time, missionaries from the universities and rest-
less spirits of the West End go into it, and learn
more or less about it, and help here, and mend
there, but they are as impotent as the man who
builds a breakwater in front of his cottage at
Seabright and thinks he has subdued the Atlantic Ocean.   They protect themselves against
certain things — *ennui* and selfishness and hard-
heartedness—but they must see in the end that
they gain more than they can give ; for where

they save one soul from the burning, two are born, still to be saved, who will breed in their turn more souls to be saved.

There is more earnest effort in the East End of London than there is, I think, in the east side of New York. I do not mean that it is more honest, but that there is more of it. This is only natural, as the need is greater, and the bitter cry of outcast London more apparent and continual than is the cry that comes from the slums of New York. I have heard several gentlemen who ought to know say that the east side of the American city is quite as appalling as is the Whitechapel of London, but I do not find it so. You cannot judge by appearances altogether; dirt and poverty, after a certain point is reached, have no degrees, and one alley looks as dark as another, and one court-yard as dirty; but you must decide by the degradation of the people, their morals, and their valuation of life, and their lack of ambition. If one judged by this the American slums would be better in comparison, although when I say " American " that is hardly fair either, as the lowest depths of degradation in New York are touched by the Italians and the Russian Jews, as it is by the latter in London, and by the English themselves.

This must necessarily be a series of *obiter dicta*, as I cannot quote in print the incidents or repeat the stories which go to prove what I say. If I

did attempt to prove it, somebody who works in
the slums would come down with a fine array of
statistics and show how wrong I was. So it
would be better to take the East End of London
from the outside entirely.

The best time to see the East End is on Sunday
morning in Petticoat Lane, and on Saturday night
in the streets which run off the Commercial Road
or Whitechapel Road, or in such alleys as Ship's
Alley, off the Ratcliff Highway. On Sunday
morning Petticoat Lane is divided into three thor-
oughfares made by two rows of handcarts, drays,
and temporary booths ranged along each gutter.
The people pass up and down these three lanes
in a long, continuous stream, which stops and con-
gests at certain points of interest and then breaks
on again. Everything that is sold, and most
things that are generally given or thrown away,
are for sale on this street on Sunday morning.
It is quite useless to enumerate them, "everything" is comprehensive enough; the fact that
they sell for nothing is the main feature of interest. It is the most excellent lesson in the
value of money that the world gives. You learn
not only the value of a penny, but the value of
a farthing. A silver sixpence shines like a diamond with the rare possibilities it presents, and
a five-pound note will buy half a mile of mer-
chandise. All of the dealers call their wares at
one and the same time, and abuse the rival deal-

ers by way of relaxation. The rival dealer does
not mind this, but regards it as a form of adver-
tisement, and answers in kind, and the crowd
listens with delighted interest. " Go on," one of
the men will cry from the back of his cart—" go
on an' buy his rotten clothes. O' course he sells
'em cheap. 'Cos why! 'Cos he never pays his
pore workin' people their waiges. He's a bloom-
ing sweater, 'e is; 'e never gives nothink to his
workers but promises and kicks; that's all 'Ammerstein gives. Yes, you do; you *know* you do.
And what 'appens, why, 'is clothes is all infected
with cholera, and falls to pieces in the sun and
shrinks up in the rain. They ain't fit for nothink
but to bury folks in, 'cos if yer moves in 'em they
falls ter pieces and leaves you naked. I don't
call no names, but this I *will* say, 'Ammerstein is
a ——— ——— ——— —— thief, 'e is, and a —— ——
—— liar, and 'is clothes is —— —— moth-eaten
cholera blankets, robbed from 'ospitals and made
over." Then "'Ammerstein," on the next cart,
who has listened to this with his thumbs in the
armholes of his waistcoat, smiles cheerfully and
says: "You musd egscuse that jail-birt on the
nexd cart. He vas a clerk of mine, but he stole
oud of der till, und I discharged him, and he feels
bat aboud id."

Saturday night is naturally the best time in
which to visit the East End, for the reason that
the men and the women have been paid off, and

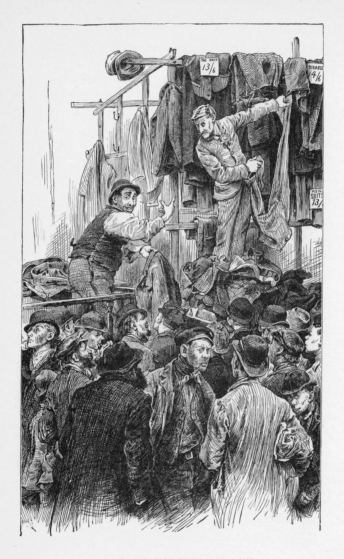

RIVAL DEALERS IN PETTICOAT LANE

are out buying the next week's rations and visiting from public-house to public-house, and are noisy and merry, or sullen and bent on fighting, as the case may be. The streets are filled with carts lit with flaring oil-lamps, and the public-houses, open on every side, are ablaze with gas and glittering with mirrors and burnished pewter, and the sausage and fish shops, with these edibles frying in the open front windows, send out broad rays of smoky light and the odor of burning fat. It is like a great out-of-door kitchen, full of wonderful colors and flaring lights and inky shadows, with glimpses of stout, florid, respectable working-men's wives, with market basket on arm, jostled by trembling hags of the river-front, and starving wild-eyed young men with enough evil purpose in their faces to do many murders, and with not enough power in their poor ill-fed and unkempt twisted bodies to strangle a child.

There are no such faces to be seen anywhere else in the world, no such despair nor misery nor ignorance.   They are brutal, sullen, and gladless. A number of these men together make you feel an uneasiness concerning your safety which is not the fear of a fellow-man, such as you might confess to if you met any men alone in a dark place, but such as you feel in the presence of an animal, an uneasiness which comes from ignorance as to what it may possibly do next, and as to how it will go about doing it.

One night an inspector of police woke fifty of these men in McCarthy's lodging-house on Dorset Street, off the Commercial Road, to exhibit them, and I felt as though I had walked into a cage with the keeper. They lay on strips of canvas naked to the waist, for it was a warm, close night, and as the ray from the policeman's lantern slid from cot to cot, it showed the sunken chests and ribs of some half-starved wrecks of the wharves, or the broad torso of a " docker," or a sailor's hairy breast marked with tattooing, and the throats of two men scarred with long, dull red lines where some one had drawn a knife. Some of them tossed and woke cursing and muttering, and then rested on their elbows, cowering before the officers and blinking at the light, or sat erect and glared at them defiantly, and hailed them with drunken bravado.

" The beds seem comfortable," I said to McCarthy, by way of being civil.

"Oh yes, sir," he answered, "comfor'ble enough, only it ain't proper, after paying twopence for your bed, to 'ave a policeman a-waking you up with a lamp in your face. It 'urts the 'ouse, that's wot it does." He added, gloomily, "It droives away trade." The most interesting group of these men I ever saw gathered together in one place was at Harwood's Music-hall. This is a place to which every stranger in London should go. It is a long, low building near Spitalfields

Market, and there are two performances a night,
one at seven and another at nine.   The price of
admittance is fourpence.   The seats are long deal
benches without arms, and the place is always
crowded with men.   I have never seen a woman
there.   The men bring their bottles of bitter ale
with them and a fried sole wrapped in paper, and
as the performance goes on they munch at the
sole in one hand and drink out of the bottle in
the other.   When a gentleman in the middle of
a bench wants more room he shoves the man
next him, and he in turn shoves the next, and
he the next, with the result that the man on the
end is precipitated violently into the aisle, to the
delight of those around him.   He takes this apparently as a matter of course, and without embarrassment or show of anger pounds the man
who has taken his end seat in the face and ribs
until he gets it again, at which this gentleman
pounds the man who had shoved him, and so it
goes on like a row of falling bricks throughout
the length of the bench.

Sometimes you will see as many as three or
four of these impromptu battles running from
bench to bench in the most orderly and good-
natured manner possible.   Harwood's has a tre-
mendous sense of humor, but the witticisms of
its *clientèle* are not translatable.   The first time
I went there we were ushered into the solitary
private box, and as our party came in, owing to

our evening dress, or to the fact that we looked down, I suppose, too curiously on the mass of evil, upturned faces, one of the boys sprang to his feet and cried: " Gentlemen, owin' to the un-expected presence of the Prince of Wailes, the audience will please rise and sing ' God save the Queen,' " which the audience did with much ironical solemnity.

The orchestra at Harwood's, which consists of five pieces, is not very good.   One night the stage-manager came before the curtain and stated that owing to the non-arrival of the sisters Bar-row, who were to do the next turn, there would be a wait of ten minutes; " this, however," he added, " will be made up to you by the gentle-men of the orchestra, who have kindly consented to play a few selections."   Instantly one of the audience jumped to his feet, and waving his hands imploringly, cried, in a voice of the keen-est fear and entreaty : " Good Gawd, governor, it 'ain't *our* fault the ladies 'aven't come.   Don't turn the orchestra on *us*.   We'll be good."

The East End of London sprang into promi-nence of late on account of the murders which were committed there.   These murders are not yet far enough off in the past to have become matters of history, nor near enough to be of " news interest."   It is not my intention to speak of them now or here, but twenty years or so from now the story of these crimes must be written,

"'OWIN' TO THE UNEXPECTED PRESENCE OF THE PRINCE OF
WAILES'"